RunIC

ASTROLOGY

About the Author

Donald Tyson is a resident of Nova Scotia, Canada. After graduating university, he developed an interest in the Tarot, which led him to study all branches of the Western esoteric tradition. His first book, *The New Magus*, was published in 1988. He has written about such varied subjects as the runes, crystal and mirror scrying, astral travel, spirit evocation, spirit familiars, the theory of magic, the Kabbalah, and the Necronomicon. He designed the popular *Necronomicon Tarot* card deck, illustrated by Anne Stokes, and is the inventor of rune dice. In his spare time he enjoys hiking, kayaking, and woodworking.

DONALD TYSON

Runic

ASTROLOGY

Chart Interpretation Through the Runes

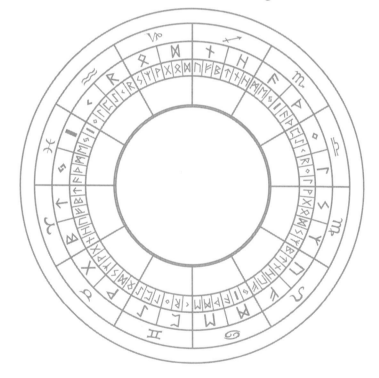

Llewellyn Publications
Woodbury, Minnesota

First Edition
First Printing, 2009

Cover art © Photodisc
Cover design by Kevin R. Brown
Editing by Sharon Leah
Llewellyn is a registered trademark of Llewellyn Worldwide, Ltd.

Library of Congress Cataloging-in-Publication Data (Pending)
ISBN: 978-0-7387-1506-3

Llewellyn Publications
A Division of Llewellyn Worldwide, Ltd.
2143 Wooddale Drive, Dept. 978-0-7387-1506-3
Woodbury, Minnesota 55125-2989, U.S.A.
www.llewellyn.com

Printed in the United States of America

Other Books by Donald Tyson

The Messenger
(Llewellyn January 1990)

Ritual Magic: What It Is & How To Do It
(Llewellyn January 1992)

Three Books of Occult Philosophy
(Llewellyn January 1992)

Scrying For Beginners
(Llewellyn February 1997)

Enochian Magic for Beginners: The Original System of Angel Magic
(Llewellyn September 2002)

Familiar Spirits: A Practical Guide for Witches & Magicians
(Llewellyn January 2004)

The Power of the Word: The Secret Code of Creation
(Llewellyn March 2004)

1-2-3 Tarot: Answers In An Instant
(Llewellyn October 2004)

Necronomicon: The Wanderings of Alhazred
(Llewellyn December 2004)

Alhazred: Author of the Necronomicon
(Llewellyn July 2006)

Portable Magic: Tarot Is the Only Tool You Need
(Llewellyn October 2006)

Soul Flight: Astral Projection and the Magical Universe
(Llewellyn March 2007)

Grimoire of the Necronomicon
(Llewellyn August 2008)

Contents

A New Kind of Oracle

Astrology is the monarch of oracles. No other system of divination approaches its level of public awareness and acceptance, as any newspaper editor who tries to pull the daily horoscope discovers when shrill letters of indignation flood in and do not stop until the horoscope is put back. Everybody knows their own Sun sign even if they do not know much else about astrology. Planetary alignments, comets, and eclipses arouse widespread interest for what they are thought to portend.

The authority of astrology may stem from its immense antiquity. Its roots are lost in the prehistory of Egypt and Mesopotamia. Exactly how old it is no one can say for certain, but the Babylonians kept meticulous records of the heavens that were purported to stretch unbroken for thousands of years, and complete astrological textbooks were being studied by the Greeks and Romans long before the birth of Christ.

More likely it is the message of oneness with the universe that makes astrology so attractive today. No matter how remote the planets and stars may appear, astrology asserts that they have a direct effect in the life of each individual. Every person is thought of as an integral note in the vast symphony of the heavenly spheres.

Despite its popularity many people shy away from the study of astrology because they consider it too difficult. It would be wonderful if a method existed to construct a horoscope that could be read strictly in keeping with the rules of astrology, but without the need to consider the geographical latitude or find Greenwich Mean Time, and without ever once having to refer to a single mathematical chart. Such a method would free the elegant interlocking symbolism of astrology, so beautiful and potent in its ancient grandeur, from the petty tyranny of a single fixed time and place. It would be possible to erect in a few minutes different charts for an individual in response to several questions, each chart completely unique even though the questions were asked in a single breath.

This is not possible in regular celestial astrology—a chart made for a specific time and place is always the same, no matter what information may be required from it. Only one pattern of the heavens exists for any given location and time on Earth—the place and moment of birth, for example. The birth chart is fixed in celestial astrology. If the time and place are not known, it is impossible to even construct a horoscope, because there is nothing in the physical universe to base it upon. This problem often arises for those who have been adopted, or whose birth records have been destroyed by fire or otherwise lost.

Astrologers will object that a chart not based upon the actual positions of the heavenly bodies is meaningless. They will say that astrology is the heavens, and the chart is no more than a way to record and represent the celestial pattern. This is a narrow view that can be disputed. The very zodiac itself is slowly rolling backwards through its signs, like a great wheel, by the phenomenon known as the precession of the equinoxes, which is caused by the wobble of our planet's axis. What are the houses but arbitrary divisions of space? There is no such thing as a house in the actual heavens. The outer planets Uranus, Neptune, and Pluto cannot even be seen with the naked eye (Uranus is barely visible under ideal seeing conditions), yet they are treated by modern astrologers as equal in importance to the inner planets, even though before 1781 (the year William Herschel discovered Uranus) they were totally unknown.

It is my own view that the stars and planets in the heavens do not exert physical influences upon human behavior and the natural world. For this reason I believe all attempts to make modern astrology more scientific by including the outer planets, or by using ever more precise measurements of position, by creating unequal house systems, and so on, are futile. Astrology was as accurate five centuries ago as it is today, perhaps more accurate.

That great student of astrology, psychoanalyst Carl Jung, acknowledged the validity of astrology, but denied that it stems from stellar and planetary positions. Referring to the precession of the equinoxes, which over time has displaced the actual signs of the zodiac from their astrological positions, Jung remarked in a letter:

> The fact that astrology nevertheless yields valid results proves that it is not the apparent positions of the stars which work, but rather the times which are measured or determined by arbitrarily named stellar positions.[1]

Although I deny the direct physical influence of the stars and planets upon our daily lives, I do not reject astrology as a system of divination. It appears to me perfectly possible that this ancient symbolic system of analysis can offer many useful insights into human nature, and even foreshadow future events and conditions. In this respect, I place astrology in exactly the same class as the I Ching, Tarot, and other oracles. To reject astrology merely because there is no physical evidence of a link between the planets and effects on Earth is to throw the baby out with the bath water. Astrology is a mental construction that functions within the psyche through the medium of symbols and their interaction. It is not a description of physical relationships between heavenly bodies.

If the symbols of the signs and planets on an astrological chart are not to be based upon the positions of the actual stars and planets in the heavens, another mechanism must be used to locate them. It must be something that carries an equal weight of authority if it is to be relied upon for answers to important questions that may affect the future lives of human beings.

The medieval scholar and astrologer Gerard Cremonensis (1114–1187) chose the sixteen symbols of geomancy, or earth-divination, to locate the planets when he devised his own system of astrological divination that was not founded upon celestial observation. He recognized the usefulness of a purely symbolic astrology, which was far greater in his day, when astrologers were forced to locate the planets using crude astronomical instruments or inaccurate outdated tables compiled centuries earlier.

In the beginning of his treatise *Of Astronomical Geomancy* he explained:

> Because Astronomy is so transcendent and subtle an Art in it self, that therein a man ought to have respect unto so many things before he can attaine to true judgement thereby, because the eye of the understanding will not pierce unto the half thereof, and few Doctors of our later time have been found so experienced therein that they know sufficiently how to judge thereby; Therefore I have composed this work, which I will have to be named *Astronomical Geomancy*; wherein, I will sufficiently teach how to judge with less labour and study. For in this present science it is not requisite to be hold neither the Ascendant, nor the hour in a Table, as it is in Astrology.[2]

Using Gerard's method it is possible to erect a legitimate, albeit an idealized, astrological chart that may be read in strict accordance with the rules of astrology. This was Gerard's purpose in creating it. The same cannot be said for a similar system of geomantic astrology invented by the occultist Henry Cornelius Agrippa (1486–1535). Agrippa's system does not result in a legitimate astrological chart, because it is possible in Agrippa's system for the same planet to occur more than once, which even in symbolic astrology is an absurdity.

Each geomantic figure is made up of four rows composed of either one or two dots. The rows are derived by randomly poking parallel lines of marks in the ground with a stick. An odd number of marks results in one dot on the corresponding row of the figure; an even number of marks generates two dots on the figure.

Geomancy enjoyed great popularity in Rome and medieval Europe. Each geomantic figure bears a Latin name and is associated with one of the seven traditional planets and one of the twelve signs of the zodiac. The antiquity of the process of selecting the figures by randomly pricking marks in the soil lends it the authority of tradition. The occult rationale was that earth spirits would direct the fall of the stick and so determine the figures.

Unfortunately, there are several things to be said against using geomancy as a mechanism for erecting astrological charts.

First, the relationship between each figure and its corresponding planet and sign appears to be arbitrary. In spite of the long tradition for this relationship, no obvious structure exists to justify it.

Second, although the correspondence between the geomantic figures and the seven planets is universally accepted, there is no similar consensus over the correspondence between the figures and the signs of the zodiac. In fact, there are at least five different systems of correspondences that have been used by various individuals or groups over the centuries that relate the zodiac to the figures of geomancy.

Third, in the methods of geomantic-generated astrology used by both Gerard and Agrippa, the accuracy of the location of a planet is limited to an entire sign—that is, a planet may be anywhere within the 30 degrees of arc occupied by the sign. This is very rough astrology indeed, and it is simply not good enough by today's standards. Even small variations in angles between planets can change the reading of a chart drastically.

Those interested in learning more about geomancy and geomantic astrology should consult Appendix VIII of my annotated edition of Agrippa's *Three Books of Occult Philosophy* (Llewellyn, 1993), where the subject is laid out in detail.

The inherent limitations of geomantic astrology have caused me to abandon the systems of both Gerard Cremonensis and Cornelius Agrippa, and create my own system of non-celestial astrology that is based upon the set of ancient Teutonic symbols known as runes.

This is possible because the runes may be structurally related to the zodiac, allowing them to indicate the placement of the planets with the accuracy of a *quine* (five degrees of arc).

The result is a symbolically correct and precise astrological chart that can be read according to astrological principles. It gains additional meaning through the consideration of the chart in conjunction with the runes by which it was formed—each rune possesses its own divinatory meaning. A third level of interpretation is available when the runes used in forming the chart are examined separately as they relate to one another.

The Ascendant, Midheaven, nodes of the Moon, and planets are located on the circle of the zodiac by selecting an equal number of runes, apparently at random, and then placing the planets upon the quines of the zodiac in the chart that are linked to those runes. The selection of runes only seems random, actually, it is no more random than any other type of divination that depends upon the guiding hand of fate. The runes are unusually potent symbols that are closely bound to the nature world and the living things of the Earth, making them ideal for divinations that rely upon *sortilege* (the practice of foretelling the future from the random fall of lots).

Over the years, I have studied all of the major traditional methods of divination. The runic astrology oracle gives the most detailed and complete response I have ever encountered. At the same time it is remarkably easy to interpret. The interconnecting structure of the horoscope acts as a framework that supports and elaborates the pithy tangible meanings of the runes. There is no end to the depth of analysis made possible by relating the runes to the signs and houses of the zodiac, coupled with the planets and their aspects. Users of this rune oracle will discover that it yields as much amplification into the details of any question as could be desired, each part of the oracle multiplying and reinforcing the meanings of all other parts.

If you are familiar with runes and the basics of astrology, you will be able to consult the oracle almost at once. If you are unfamiliar with astrology or the runes, you will find all the information you need to interpret a runic astrology chart in the following chapters.

Because runic astrology works unhindered by the tyranny of the heavens, no mathematical calculations, tables, or number charts of any kind are ever needed. All that is necessary is an understanding of the meanings and relationships of astrological symbols, and a knowledge of the divinatory significance of the twenty-four Germanic runes. A runic astrology chart can be cast for anyone at any time and in any place without the need to know where or when that person was born, or indeed anything at all about the individual seeking the reading.

All the information to erect a full runic astrology chart is right here in this book. There are two instruments, runic cards and dice, which are separate and complete rune oracles in their own right, that are used in runic astrology to select the positions of astrological components on the zodiac. The dice and cards streamline the process of setting up the chart, and both can be easily constructed from inexpensive and readily available materials. This book is all you need to make the runic astrology oracle a part of your life.

2

Runes on the Zodiac

Runes are graphic symbols used by the ancient Teutonic peoples of northern Europe for magic and written communication. Each rune is both an occult sigil representing a god or power of nature, and the letter of an alphabet. When they are used as letters they form intelligible words and convey messages that are usually quite straightforward and simple. When they are used for magical purposes, they often appear unintelligible but are grouped in numerical series with single runes repeated significant numbers of times.

Since both types of inscriptions occur on the same artifacts side by side, the unintelligible rune series cannot be dismissed as illiterate copying; it must possess a clear magical intent, even though any occult significance is seldom understood by modern rune scholars. Occasionally the scribal and magical functions are combined in magic words of power such as the word *alu* (taboo), or the names of gods such as Woden and Thor.

Magically, runes were used both in an active way to cause specific changes in human beings and the natural world, and in a passive way to divine the future and reveal secret or hidden matters. Traces of these two roots of rune magic survive in historical accounts by the Roman and early Christian writers, and in Scandinavian, Icelandic and Old English poetry, but they are nowhere described in precise physical detail.

This is not the place to give the complete story of the fascinating evolution of runes, which has been examined in depth in the second chapter of my book *Rune Magic*.[1] But briefly, the runes were born around 500 BC in northern Italy, the result of a magical marriage between the occult symbols used by Teutonic shamans in their rituals, and the letters of the Etruscan alphabet. They quickly spread throughout northern Europe, extending as

Aettir	Runes	German		English		Meanings
		Names	Sounds	Names	Sounds	
ᚠ	ᚠ	Fehu	f	Feoh	f	Cattle
	ᚢ	Uruz	u	Ur	u	Aurochs
	ᚦ	Thurisaz	th	Thorn	th	Devil
	ᚨ	Ansuz	a	Os	o	God
	ᚱ	Raido	r	Rad	r	Riding
	ᚲ	Kano	k	Cen	c	Torch
	ᚷ	Gebo	g	Gyfu	g	Gift
	ᚹ	Wunjo	w	Wyn	w	Glory
ᚺ	ᚺ	Hagalaz	h	Haegl	h	Hail
	ᚾ	Nauthiz	n	Nyd	n	Need
	ᛁ	Isa	I	Is	I	Ice
	ᛃ	Jera	j	Ger	j	Harvest
	ᛇ	Eihwaz	ei	Eoh	eo	Yew
	ᛈ	Perth	p	Peordh	p	Apple
	ᛉ	Algiz	z	Eolh	x	Defense
	ᛊ	Sowelu	s	Sigel	s	Sun
ᛏ	ᛏ	Teiwaz	t	Tir	t	Courage
	ᛒ	Berkana	b	Beorc	b	Birch
	ᛖ	Ehwaz	e	Eh	e	Horse
	ᛗ	Mannaz	m	Man	m	Man
	ᛚ	Laguz	l	Lagu	l	Water
	ᛜ	Inguz	ng	Ing	ng	Fertility
	ᛞ	Dagaz	d	Daeg	d	Day
	ᛟ	Othila	o	Ethel	oe	Homeland

Figure 2-1

far as Russia in the east and Iceland in the west. They were carried even farther afield by the Vikings in their restless wanderings.

The oldest rune alphabet, and the purest magically, is the elder German futhark of twenty-four runes. Futhark is a word coined from the first six runes of this alphabet: F, U, Th, A, R, K. The third rune has a "th" sound in English but it is a single rune letter. From the German futhark diverged the rune alphabets used in England and Scandinavia. In England the number of runes was first extended to twenty-eight, and later in Northumbria to thirty-three. At the same time in Denmark, Sweden, and Norway the runes were reduced in number to sixteen.

Only the elder German futhark is considered here. It is the purest rune alphabet, preserving the original groupings of the runes intact, and it is the nearest to the magical meanings of the rune symbols. When rune magic was at its height in the early centuries of the present era, it was worked with the elder futhark. The very forms of the German runes, composed entirely of vertical and diagonal strokes, reflect the practice of cutting them with a sharp blade into wood across its grain for occult purposes. Horizontal strokes were avoided because woodgrain running the same way as the stroke was apt to obscure the mark, and also, cutting with the grain instead of across it ran the risk of splintering or splitting the wood. Later alphabets contain degenerate rune forms with horizontal and rounded strokes. These rune forms evolved after runes were commonly engraved into stone and metal, or penned on parchment, all surfaces that lacked strong grain.

It is important to gain familiarity with the shapes, names, and meanings of individual runes before attempting to use them for divination. The runes, their names and sounds in both German and English, and the basic meanings of their names appear in Figure 2-1 for quick reference. Most people use the German names for the twenty-four runes of the German futhark. For these reasons, the German names have been used here when referring to the elder runes.

There is no ancient assignment of these twenty-four runes to the zodiac, the planets, and the occult elements. Even so, the runes can be linked individually with the seven traditional planets of astrology, the twelve signs, and the five elements (counting the quintessence as an element) based upon their separate natures. In Appendix A, I have presented my personal set of correspondences. These were made by considering each rune in turn and judging which of the signs, planets, or elements best matched its qualities. No underlying common structure between the futhark and these three sets of astrological symbols exists that may be used as a guide, and therefore these correspondences must be regarded as tentative.

The futhark does, however, have an ancient and inherent structure that allows it to be assigned with confidence to the zodiac, and rationally distributed in a great ring around the heavens. This underlying structure must be explained in detail because it is the basis for runic astrology. The futhark is built upon two essential divisions. The first is universally recognized, and the second, although not beyond dispute, is strongly supported by internal evidence.

The twenty-four runes are divided into three *aettir* (families) of eight runes. Each aett is named after the rune that begins it, which may be regarded as the patriarch of the family it heads. This trine of families was so important that it survived the increase of the runes in England and the decrease in their number that occurred in Scandinavia. The three aettir are the Fehu aett, the Hagalaz aett, and the Teiwaz aett.

The relationship between the aettir and qualities of astrology can be tabulated this way:

Fehu aett: fixed (♌ , ♏ , ♒ , ♉)

Hagalaz aett: mutable (♐ , ♓ , ♊ , ♍)

Tiewaz aett: cardinal (♈ , ♋ , ♎ , ♑)

The association between the families of the runes and the *quadruplicities* (groups of four signs) of the zodiac is determined by the nature of the naming rune that begins each aett and acts as the keynote of its collective quality. Fehu is the rune for cattle, and by extension, moveable possessions. It is material and passive, corresponding to the physical level in humanity, and the fixed signs in astrology. Hagalaz is the rune for hail, symbolizing the violent forces of nature. It is wild and destructive, capricious in its effects and unconscious both of the source and outcome of its actions, corresponding well with the emotional level in humanity, and the mutable signs in astrology. Teiwaz is the rune for honor, truth, and courage, the virtues of the intellect. It corresponds with the conscious level in humanity, and the cardinal signs in astrology. Thus, Fehu is acted upon, Hagalaz interacts and reacts, and Teiwaz acts.

The second essential division of the futhark is into twelve rune pairs. Each rune is related in some meaningful way with its adjacent pair-rune. There are four rune pairs in each aett. The existence of these rune pairs is not universally recognized by scholars but seems inescapable when the meanings of the individual runes are compared.

Pair relationships may be contrasting or complementary. For example, Fehu (ᚠ), the domestic cow, contrasts with Uruz (ᚢ), the aurochs, a type of fierce wild ox. Thurisaz (ᚦ), an

	Fire	Water	Air	Earth	
Fehu aett	ᚠᚢ	ᚦᚨ	ᚱᚲ	ᚷᚹ	Fixed
Hagalaz aett	ᚺᛏ	ᛁᛇ	ᛃᛈ	ᛇᛉ	Mutable
Teiwaz aett	ᛏᛒ	ᛗᛖ	ᛚᛜ	ᛝᛟ	Cardinal
	1st cube	2nd cube	3rd cube	4th cube	

Figure 2-2

evil giant or demon, contrasts with Ansuz (ᚨ), a wise and benevolent god. On the other hand, Raido (ᚱ), a journey on horseback, or quest, is complemented and completed by Kano (ᚲ), a guiding light or beacon. Gebo (ᚷ), a gift or sacrifice, is complemented by Wunjo (ᚹ), joy or glory.

It is natural to relate the four pairs in each aett to the four elements of fire, water, air, and earth. This ordering of the elements is indicated by the way they appear upon the zodiac in each of the three quadruplicities. In the cardinal group of signs, for example, fire-sign Aries is followed in the usual counterclockwise direction of motion by water-sign Cancer, air-sign Libra, and earth-sign Capricorn. The same pattern of elements repeats itself in the four fixed and four mutable signs.

It is natural to begin with the fire signs in each quadruplicity because fire is almost universally recognized as the first of the four elements. Very rarely air is placed above fire, but this is uncommon.

These two essential divisions of the futhark, and the way they cause the runes to fall under the influence of the three qualities and four elements, are clearly displayed in Figure 2-2.

The three pairs of runes under each element—one pair from each family—are inscribed upon one of the four rune dice. Pair-runes occupy opposite faces of each cube. It is important to know the arrangement of runes upon the dice in order to understand how they function in the oracle. The placement of the runes on the dice is described in the next chapter. I invented these dice for rune divination many years ago. Prior to their use in the *Runic Astrology*, they were included in my *Power of the Runes* kit, and also in my *Rune Dice* divination kit.

The first pair ᚠ-ᚢ is placed on the fixed-fire-sign Leo. Following the traditional order of the signs counterclockwise, the second rune pair ᚦ-ᚨ is placed on the fixed-water-sign, Scorpio; the third pair ᚱ-ᚲ is placed on the fixed-air-sign Aquarius; and the fourth pair ᚷ-ᚹ is placed on the fixed-earth-sign Taurus. The second and third aettir are located on the mutable and cardinal signs in the same way.

By applying the twenty-four runes directly to the zodiac, each rune rules and influences a *quindecan* (half a sign, or 15 degrees). A further six-fold division of the sign is possible by applying the six runes under each element to the six *quines* (faces), which are divisions of 5 degrees. The method is simple. Array the three pairs of runes under the element of each zodiac sign in order counterclockwise, filling the six faces of the sign. Always begin with the first rune of the pair that rules the sign.

For example, Leo is a fire sign. The six runes that occupy its quines are the fire runes. Since the first rune of the pair that rules Leo is Fehu (ᚠ), the fire runes are arrayed counterclockwise on Leo in this order: ᚠ, ᚢ, ᚺ, ᛏ, ᛉ, ᛒ. Pisces is a water sign. The first pair-rune of Pisces is Isa (ᛁ). Therefore, the six water runes are arrayed counterclockwise on Pisces in this order: ᛁ, ᛜ, ᛗ, ᛖ, ᚦ, ᚨ. The same rule is applied to all the signs until the seventy-two quines are filled with three complete rune alphabets (24 X 3 = 72), one futhark for each quadruplicity of signs.

The whole structure of the runic zodiac can be seen in the accompanying diagram, Figure 2-3, which forms the large chart of the oracle.

Figure 2-3

3

Tools of Runic Astrology

When using the runic astrology oracle to tell the fortunes of friends or clients, you will need a deck of twenty-four rune cards, a set of four rune dice, a large colored chart of the rune zodiac, and a set of counters that are placed upon it to mark the locations of the planets and other astrological indicators. The large chart is designed to display the horoscope in a clear and visually appealing way so that it can easily be interpreted for others. You will also need a small blank chart of the rune zodiac on which to record the details of the horoscope for a permanent record.

All of these components are clearly illustrated in this book. You can construct the necessary items yourself, doing as finished and attractive a job as you feel to be appropriate for your own use. This chapter will describe how to make them.

Make Your Own Cards

A rough but serviceable deck of rune cards can be made very easily from small filing cards. The best cards to use are the unlined kind, and the smaller they are, the better, since the smaller filing cards are easier to shuffle and lay out. Mark a large rune in red ink on one side of each so that it fills most of the card. A red felt marker with a broad tip will do the job. It is best if you can get filing cards thick enough so that you cannot see the runes through the backs—this will help you to make a truly random selection from the cards.

The best medium for handmade rune cards is a set of blank tarot cards, which tarot card retailers and producers sometimes offer for sale to those wishing to draw and color their own tarot cards. A blank set of tarot cards contains eighty blank cards (two more than the standard seventy-eight-card tarot deck), which will give you more than three times the number of cards you need to make a rune card deck. The extra cards are useful to have, since they allow you to make two decks—an everyday set of rune cards for rough use, and a fine set of rune cards to keep for special divinations—or to replace cards that get damaged or lost. A number of resources are available online for blank cards.

Make Your Own Rune Dice

If you do not possess a set of my rune dice, it is easy to make your own set. Go to a craft store such as Michaels and buy a package of hardwood cubes that are each ¾ inch in size, or as near to that size as you can get. These cubes of wood are usually very accurately made and well sanded. If you are unable to locate blank wood cubes in a store near you, there are a number of Internet sites that offer blank wood cubes at very low prices.

With a red pen or marker, draw the six runes of each elemental set on the six sides of the cube, taking care to place the runes of each rune pair on opposite sides of the cube. That is to say, the runes of the first elemental pair of fire, Fehu-Uruz, would be marked on the front and the back; the runes of the second elemental pair of fire, Hagalaz-Nauthiz, would be marked on the top and the bottom; the runes of the third elemental pair of fire, Teiwaz-Berkana, would be marked on the left and the right. And so on for the rune pairs of the other elemental sets. This will give you a workable set of rune dice. You can make the dice out of any convenient material, but the prefinished cubes of hardwood sold by craft stores and on the Internet are inexpensive and work very well.

Rune dice can also be made very easily from four large regular dice. If you do use regular dice, cover their facets with adhesive labels, then mark the appropriate rune upon each face. The runes should be marked with red ink. Red is the color of blood, and in an esoteric sense is the lifeforce that feeds the runes and gives them their power. If you wish, you may use colored pencils to shade each die the color that matches its element to help distinguish it from the others. Shade the fire die pale red, the water die pale blue, the air die yellow, and the earth die pale green.

There is a specific orientation of the runes upon the dice that must be imitated if they are to be properly made. Scan, photocopy, or redraw the models of the dice (Figure 3-1), which show the six sides expanded and laid flat. Cut them out, then fold each one together into a cube, holding it in place with transparent sticky tape. By referring to them, you will be sure to get the pattern of each elemental die correct. Be sure to follow the patterns ex-

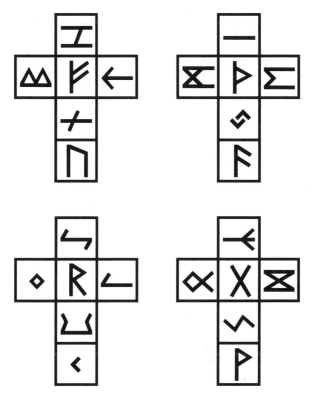

Figure 3-1

actly, not only putting the correct rune on each facet of the dice, but also aligning the runes in the manner shown.

In a pinch, when you want to cast a runic astrology chart but do not have a set of rune dice on hand, a single regular die marked with dots can substitute for the set of rune dice. The purpose of the rune dice is to pinpoint specific quines within the signs of the zodiac. When an ordinary die is used in place of a rune die, it is necessary to count counterclockwise the number of quines in the sign corresponding with the number of spots that turns up on the die. This locates one of the six quine-runes in the sign. It is a poor substitute for the rune dice, which reveal the quines of the planets directly when they are cast, but it is a workable alternative.

Make Your Own Rune Zodiac Diagram

If you wish to do readings for others in such a way that the runic astrology oracle is attractively displayed, you must make a copy of the large chart that is illustrated at the end of the second chapter. The easiest way is to scan it from the book, then print it to as large a size as you can manage. If you take the scanned file in to a copy shop, they will probably have an oversized copier that is able to do copies larger than a standard letter page. Or you might want to print out the large chart in two halves on legal-sized pages, and then join them together along the back with tape. This will result in a zodiac circle almost fourteen inches in diameter. You can always draw the chart by hand on a sheet of bristol board or good quality drawing paper, so that the circle of the zodiac is from 18 to 24 inches in diameter. If you draw the large chart yourself, mark the runes in red.

It is not difficult to draw accurate large circles if you place your paper upon a sheet of plywood or other firm surface. Drive a pin or small nail into the center of the sheet, then use a loop of button thread over this center pin to guide your pencil in a circle. You can change the diameter of the circle by shortening or lengthening the loop of thread. A long, thin stick, such as a yardstick, with a hole at one end for a pivot and a series of holes drilled at the appropriate distance through which to insert your pencil, is even more accurate as a radius when scribing these circles. A protractor can then be used to divide off the degrees of the signs, quindecans, and quines.

The spaces occupied by the zodiac signs, quindecan runes, and quine runes are shaded in their elemental colors using colored pencils. The shading must not be so heavy that it obscures the signs or runes. The four elemental triangles at the quarters take the color of the sign closest to them, and should be shaded in as follows:

Leo, Sagittarius, Aries—red (fire)

Scorpio, Pisces, Cancer—blue (water)

Aquarius, Gemini, Libra—yellow (air)

Taurus, Virgo, Capricorn—green (earth)

The background of the first rune of each quindecan in a sign, counting counterclockwise, takes the shading of the sign, but the second quindecan rune is shaded the opposite elemental color. The runes of the quines similarly alternate—the first quine is shaded the elemental color of the sign, the second quine its opposite, the third quine the elemental color, the fourth quine its opposite, and so on. Red is opposite yellow; green is opposite blue.

For example, Libra is shaded light yellow. Moving counterclockwise, the first quindecan, Laguz (ᛚ), is also shaded yellow, but the other quindecan, Inguz (ᛜ), is shaded the opposite color, red. The first quine of Libra, Laguz, is yellow; the second quine, Inguz, is red; the third quine, Raido (ᚱ), is yellow; the fourth quine, Kano (ᚲ), is red; the fifth quine, Eihwaz (ᛇ), is yellow; and the sixth quine, Perth (ᛈ), is red.

The same color scheme is carried through for all the signs, so that each sign along with the runes under it bears its own elemental color and also the color of its opposite sign. Be sure the red shading is applied lightly over the red runes so that the runes are not obscured—it should be a pink or coral color. Colored pencils work well.

The easiest way to make a rough set of counters for the Ascendant, planets, and North (ascending) Node of the Moon is to cover pennies on one side with a plain adhesive label and trim off the excess with scissors, then mark on them the astrological symbols with a black pen or marker. Any set of small, flat disks upon which you can mark or paint the glyphs will serve for the counters. It will help to further distinguish these counters at a glance if you use colored pencils to shade them with the following colors:

Component	Symbol	Color
Ascendant	A	White
Moon	☽	Silver
Mercury	☿	Orange
Venus	♀	Green
Sun	☉	Gold
Mars	♂	Red
Jupiter	♃	Blue
Saturn	♄	Black
North Node	☊	Purple

It is also necessary to have a smaller blank chart upon which to record the planetary positions, aspects, and runes displayed on the large chart that make up the horoscope. This is referred to when obtaining a more detailed analysis than is possible in the short time that may be available for a direct person-to-person reading from the large chart. The smaller chart creates a permanent record of the divination that may be filed away and consulted years after the initial reading. When an in-depth reading is done for a friend or client, the

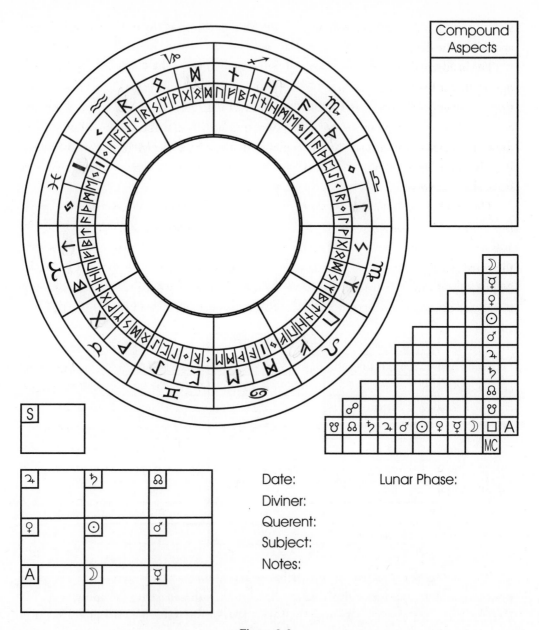

Figure 3-2

small chart should be explained and then given to that person along with a detailed written analysis of the divination.

The blank chart used in runic astrology differs from the usual blank sold for regular astrology, in that it has the double circle of the runes inscribed within the zodiac, and an empty ring for recording the position of the houses outside the zodiac. It may be possible to modify a standard blank chart by marking the runes upon it, but it will make a clearer display if you draw or scan the example and print up copies so that you have enough blanks for your readings. If you retain your master copy in a safe place, you can photocopy or scan more blank small charts as you need them.

The small chart provides spaces for only the seven planets of traditional astrology. This is the chart I use in my own work, on the principle that if seven planets were enough in astrology for five thousand years, they are enough for me. For others who want to include the three outer planets in divinations, it is an easy matter to mark the glyphs for Uranus, Neptune, and Pluto on the chart. The three outer planets may be located on the circle of the zodiac in the same way that the other planets are located, by using the rune cards and rune dice. Simply lay out an additional row of three rune cards above the rest, one card each for the three outer planets. In my opinion, this additional complexity is unnecessary.

If you intend to do runic astrology just for yourself and a few friends, and are not concerned about making a dramatic visual display for clients, you will find that only the small chart is necessary. Instead of placing the counters on the large chart to mark the positions of the planets, the planet glyphs can be drawn directly in their places on the small chart as their positions are located with the cards and dice. Construction of the large chart and the ten counters is optional for those who often do runic astrology for others, and who wish to explain the chart as it is in the process of being laid out.

How to Use the Oracle

To consult the runic astrology oracle using the large chart, you need a table or other clean, flat surface. Spread the large color chart on the table with the green triangle of earth on your left hand and the red triangle of fire on your right. A chair should be ready for the querent—the person asking the question—on the opposite side of the chart.

Shuffle the deck of rune cards thoroughly to mix them. You do not need to worry about whether they are upright or inverted, since inversions of the rune cards are not taken into account during the reading. Runic astrology has enough complexity without considering reversals of the runes. If you wish to consider reversals, you may do so, but it is unnecessary. When the cards are well mixed, lay the deck face down in the center of the zodiac circle on the large chart.

Position the rune dice on the triangles at the four corners of the chart. The die with the fire runes is set in the red triangle next to the sign Leo; the die with the water runes in the blue triangle next to Scorpio; the die with the air runes in the yellow triangle next to Aquarius; the die with the earth runes, in the green triangle next to Taurus. Check to see that you have placed these dice correctly. The runes on each die should be the same as the runes in the quines of the sign adjacent to its elemental triangle.

Arrange the following counters in a straight line along the edge of the chart nearest to you, or in a line up the right side:

$$A \; ☽ \; ☿ \; ♀ \; ☉ \; ♂ \; ♃ \; ♄ \; ☊$$

Make sure you have enough space to the left of the large chart to lay out the rune cards. Also keep somewhere near at hand a blank copy of the small chart and a pencil or pen for entering the positions of the planets, houses, Ascendant, Midheaven, lunar nodes, and aspects. You are now ready to begin the reading.

Ask the querent the subject of the divination. As the querent explains the matter into which he or she wishes to gain insight, remain receptive. It is best at this stage not to try to form intellectual judgments about the personality of the querent or the nature of the question, but to stay passive and absorb impressions below the level of conscious thought. This awakens the intuitive faculty and permits it to guide your interpretation of the chart.

Take up the cards and shuffle them lightly while passively considering the querent. Then set the cards back in the center of the chart and ask the querent to cut them once. Traditionally, in divination, cards are cut to the left with the left hand, but this is not really important. Put the lower part of the deck back onto the upper part following the cut and take off the uppermost card, turning it up to reveal the rune as you do so.

The card the querent has cut from the deck is the Significator rune. It acts as the keynote of the reading and is the rune to which all other runes are related for significance. Enter the rune glyph on the small chart in the box provided for it.

Put the Significator back in the deck and pass the cards to the querent to be shuffled. Tell the querent to concentrate on the subject of the reading as the cards are mixed. When the querent feels satisfied the cards have been shuffled enough, tell the querent to set the deck in the center of the chart and cut it yourself once, then take up the cards and deal out nine of them face down in three rows of three to the left of the chart in the order shown in Figure 4-1. Each card is linked with one of the counters, as you can see by examining the boxes on the lower left corner of the small chart. The rune on the card places the counter related to it in its correct sign on the zodiac.

Turn the first card (the one at the lower left of the group) face up. The rune revealed on the first card locates the sign of the Ascendant. Find the rune on the circle of twenty-four quindecans that matches the rune on the card. Whichever sign this rune occupies, that is the Ascendant sign.

To locate the exact quine of the Ascendant, determine the element of the Ascendant sign, which is the same as the element of the rune on the Ascendant card. Take up the single die of that element, have the querent blow lightly on the die to make an occult link between the die and the querent, then cast it upon the center of the chart. Place the counter of the Ascendant within its sign upon the rune that is uppermost on the die. Return the die to its

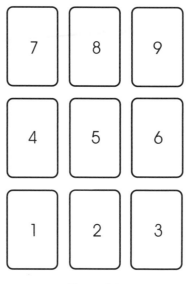

Figure 4-1

triangle. The exact degree of the Ascendant is the first degree of its quine, proceeding in the usual counterclockwise direction.

The process of placing the counters may be a bit hard to follow in the abstract, but an example should make it clear. Let us say the first rune card you turn up bears the Raido (R) rune. This means the Ascendant will be located somewhere within the sign Aquarius, because Raido is in Aquarius on the circle of the twenty-four quindecan runes. To determine which of the six quines of Aquarius the Ascendant falls upon, take up the die of air, which rests upon the yellow triangle, have the querent blow upon it, and cast it in the center of the chart. The air die is used because Aquarius is an air sign. Continuing the example, if the rune Inguz (◇) turns up on the air die, the counter marking the degree of the Ascendant (A) is put on the sixth quine of Aquarius, which is marked on the chart by the Inguz rune.

Because the Midheaven, or *Medium Coeli* (MC), is related to the Ascendant, in runic astrology it is always placed in a square aspect, or right angle (90 degrees), clockwise from the quine of the Ascendant. It is not necessary to cast a rune die to find the quine of Midheaven. It should be noted that in regular astrology charts the Midheaven is not always at a perfect right angle to the Ascendant (under most systems of astrology), but varies somewhat due to the tilt and the motions of the planet Earth. However, runic astrology does not rely on a measurement of the actual positions of the stars and planets in the heavens, so the idealized location of the Midheaven, at a right angle to the Ascendant, is used.

In our example, since Aquarius is the sign of the Ascendant, Scorpio must be the sign of Midheaven, since it is at a square aspect (90-degree right angle) clockwise with Aquarius. The Ascendant is in the sixth quine of Aquarius, that of Inguz (◇); consequently, the sixth quine of Scorpio, that of Mannaz (ᛗ), must be the location of Midheaven.

Turn the second card, which is the middle card in the bottom row, face up. The cards are exposed in the same sequence they were laid out. Locate the rune of the second card on the circle of the quindecans and take note of its sign. This is the zodiac sign in which the Moon resides for this reading. Extend to the querent the elemental die that corresponds with the element of the sign of the Moon, and have the querent blow upon it, then cast it to determine which of the six quines of that sign the counter of the Moon is placed on. Position the counter of the Moon and put the rune die back on its triangle. Always replace the dice on their triangles so that you do not mix them up.

The remaining planets are located upon the inner ring of the seventy-two quines in the same way. The rune cards determines the signs; the rune dice determine the quines. The reason for asking the querent to blow upon the dice before casting them is to establish an occult link through the breath between the dice and the question of the divination. In the Western esoteric tradition, the living breath has always been considered a manifest expression of the spirit. Gamblers blow on dice for good luck. Unconsciously, they are calling upon the force of their spirit to influence the fall of the dice. This superstition has a real basis in Western magic, which we make use of during rune divination.

Following the Ascendant and Midheaven quines, the seven traditional planets are located upon the chart in their order of apparent rapidity of motion as viewed from the Earth: Moon, Mercury, Venus, Sun, Mars, Jupiter, and Saturn. This order has been recognized in astrology since ancient times, and is referred to as the Ptolemaic order, after the great second-century Greek astronomer Claudius Ptolemaeus, who expounded upon it in complex detail in his work.[1] Since the Ascendant and Midheaven positions are both tied to the Earth, there is an unbroken chain in this sequence of planets from the Earth at the center to Saturn at the outer limit. This order of the planets does not correspond with the true structure of the solar system, but from a geocentric point of view, where the observer is considered to be the center of the universe, it makes sense.

Turn up the ninth and final card to determine the placements of the two lunar nodes, the North Node, or Dragon's Head (☊), and the South Node, or Dragon's Tail (☋). Only the North Node need be located on the large chart by using its rune card and corresponding elemental die—the South Node is always exactly opposite the North Node on the circle of the zodiac. For example, if the last rune card is Gebo (**X**), the North Node will be in Taurus; and if the cast of the earth die that is linked to Taurus turns up the rune Sowelu (**ϟ**), the counter for the North Node will occupy the fourth quine of Taurus. The South Node is then directly opposite on the fourth quine of Scorpio, which happens to be occupied by Jera (**ϟ**). The positions of the Midheaven and South Node should be marked on the small chart, but it is not really necessary to have a counter to fix them on the large chart, since they are located by the Ascendant and the North (ascending) Node, respectively.

After the large chart has been erected, you may wish to make an initial verbal interpretation in the presence of the querent, explaining the structure and meaning of the chart graphically by indicating the positions of the counters and the meanings of their relationships. If the reading is casual there may be no need to record the result on the small chart, but if the reading is to be done in depth for a more serious purpose, you must enter the information conveyed by the rune cards and the large chart into the appropriate spaces provided on the small blank chart.

The places of the Ascendant, Midheaven, lunar nodes, and planets are marked on the small chart with their symbol glyphs in the wide-open circle that lies within the ring of the rune quines. I like to orientate the symbols so that they are upright when considered from the point of view of the center of the zodiac, but this is not an important matter. The glyphs of planets in conjunction should be marked one above the other and beneath the rune quine they share.

As a practical matter, it is a good idea to record all information on the small chart first in light pencil, so that if you make a mistake you can erase and correct it without ruining the chart. Later the data can be more carefully entered upon the chart in red, blue, and black inks, which make an attractive presentation.

Small marks are made on the circumference of the inner circle directly below the planets and other significant degrees, and straight lines drawn between them to show the astrological aspects. Easy aspects—trine, sextile, and some conjunctions—are marked in blue; difficult aspects—square, opposition, and some conjunctions—are marked in red. Although it is not the common astrological practice, I like to mark in the aspects of the nodes of the Moon to remind myself that they are significant factors in the chart.

The triangular grid on the lower right of the small chart is designed to record the aspects in symbolic form. If an aspect exists between two planets it is entered into the box where the row and column of those planets cross. Aspects with the Ascendant are entered up the right-hand side of the grid; aspects with the Midheaven are entered along the bottom. The box marked Compound Aspects above the aspect grid may be used for aspects that involve more than two planets or other significant points such as the nodes.

The degree of the Ascendant, which is the first degree of the quine the Ascendant occupies, locates the cusp, or beginning, of the first house. In runic astrology, the houses are considered to occupy equal arcs of 30 degrees, in a way similar to the equal house system of regular astrology. The twelve houses are indicated by dividing the empty outer ring into twelve equal parts, starting from the degree of the Ascendant. The resulting houses are labeled in Roman numerals from I to XII, beginning with the house of the Ascendant and proceeding counterclockwise.

Those familiar with common astrology charts will notice that in the usual chart, houses are permanently printed on the blank chart, and the signs are marked in later in relation to the houses. In this way the Ascendant always appears midway up the left side of the chart. Because of the need to indicate the runes on the zodiac, in the runic astrology chart it is the signs that are printed on the blank chart in a fixed position, and the Ascendant and houses that are variably placed. It is only the relationship between houses and signs that is important, so both these approaches work equally well.

The runes upon the nine selected rune cards should be noted in the nine boxes provided for this purpose on the small chart by drawing a single large rune in red ink in each box. If reversals of the rune cards are ignored, as is the usual practice for runic astrology, draw these runes in an upright position even if they happen to be inverted on the cards that are turned. You will have already entered the significator rune in the separate box provided for it.

At the bottom right of the chart note the date of the reading, the phase of the Moon, the name of the diviner (yourself), the name of the querent, and the general subject of the reading. Under Notes enter any factors in the chart that strike you as especially significant.

The phase of the Moon reveals whether the reading was done during a favorable or unfavorable period. The waxing and Full Moon are considered to help, while the waning and dark Moon are thought to hinder. I indicate the lunar phase by dividing it into first, second, third, and fourth quarters to stand for the periods from New Moon to half-full, half-full to full, Full Moon to half-empty, and half-empty to New Moon. The three days bracketing the Full Moon (day before, day of the Full Moon, and the day after) I mark as full, and the three days around the New Moon I mark new.

The sample readings in chapters fifteen and sixteen show clearly how all the relevant information is to be entered upon the small chart. Use them as your guide until you gain familiarity with the process of recording the runic astrology data and no longer need to refer to them.

Meanings of the Runes

Each rune can be interpreted on several different levels. The level of meaning that applies in any given circumstance is determined by context. Often, more than one interpretation is possible at the same time. All meanings of the runes, from the tangible to the abstract, stem from their root meanings that are embodied in their names.

Favorable or unfavorable position is determined by the placement of the rune in its sign and house, the planet that falls upon it, and the aspects influencing it. An unfavorable placement of a rune does not always signify a negative influence, but may merely mean that the action of the rune is hindered or weakened.

 ## Fehu: Cattle

In ancient times, as in primitive cultures of the present day, cattle represented units of value. The wealth of a person was determined by how many cattle and slaves he or she owned.

Literal: Livestock

Symbolic: Valuable possession

Anthropomorphic: A merchant

Favorably Placed

Moveable possessions, money, wealth, a precious object, increase in income, important purchase, payment of debt, luxury, opulence, power through money, generosity

Unfavorably Placed

Slavery, dependence, bondage to material things, greed, miserliness, cowardice, lack of imagination, stupidity, subservience, a victim mentality, manual labor, poverty

Key: Possession

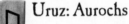 # Uruz: Aurochs

The aurochs, which is now extinct, was a wild beast similar to a great shaggy ox and with the irascible disposition of a bear. It was covered in long black hair and had curled, ram-like horns. The young warriors of northern Europe hunted it as a test of manhood.

Literal: Wild ox

Symbolic: Male virility

Anthropomorphic: A soldier

Favorably Placed

Strength, courage, boldness, vitality, sexual potency, freedom, enterprise, dominance, leadership, martial skills

Unfavorably Placed

Rashness, violence, brutality, immaturity, lust, lack of control, unpreparedness, callousness, criminal behavior

Key: Action

 # Thurisaz: Devil

Thurisaz is the personal name of an evil giant described as the "torturer of women." Probably one of the frost giants who battled the gods of Asgard. The embodiment of all that is base, cowardly and wicked.

Literal: An evil devil

Symbolic: Cruelty

Anthropomorphic: An enemy

Favorably Placed

Nemesis, poetic justice, purging, catharsis, exposure of malice, falling into one's own trap, just deserts, an evil from which good results, attempt to do harm will backfire

Unfavorably Placed

Malice, lies, vindictiveness, cowardly spite, persecution, envy, jealousy, hatred, deceit, torture, wickedness for its own sake

> *Key:* Evil

Ansuz: Wise God

This is the father of the gods, Wotan to the Germans and Odin to the Norse, whose wisdom flowed from his mouth like a river.

Literal: A benevolent god

Symbolic: Good counsel

Anthropomorphic: An authority figure

Favorably Placed

Wisdom, true words, instruction, eloquence, helpful communication, important message, loving actions, harmony, personal insight, benevolence, protection

Unfavorably Placed

Rigidity, control, obsession with order, fussiness, concern for details, pomposity, authoritarianism, a mother hen, inability to delegate authority, verbosity, punctiliousness

> *Key:* Goodness

Raido: Journey by Horse

An extended land journey, which in ancient times was always undertaken on horseback. By extension, a spiritual quest after enlightenment.

Literal: Travel on horse

Symbolic: Quest

Anthropomorphic: A stranger

Favorably Placed

Relocation, vacation, change of address, business trip, travel, treasure hunt, personal evolution, quest for enlightenment, escape from evil

Unfavorably Placed

Disruption, dislocation, forced removal, flight from responsibility, journey into darkness, aimlessness, wandering, empty ambitions, chasing rainbows, lack of fulfillment, long illness, possible death

    Key: Journey

 ## Kano: Torch

A man-made flame such as a torch, lantern or bonfire that illuminates the darkness. By extension, the light of the mind that guides human actions.

Literal: Guiding flame

Symbolic: Light of spirit

Anthropomorphic: A messenger

Favorably Placed

Guidance, direction, revelation, illumination, reason, answer, goal, light in darkness, the mind, realization, solution to a problem

Unfavorably Placed

Exposure, naked truth, realization of futility, loss of hope, shattered dreams, awakening to reality, cold light of day, broken promise, awareness of personal limitations, news of a death, possible suicide attempt

    Key: Beacon

 ## Gebo: Gift

A voluntary sacrifice undertaken to attain a greater purpose. This may be a material gift to win the favor of an individual or the sacrifice upon an altar to a higher spiritual power.

Literal: Gift or offering

Symbolic: Sacrifice of the lower for the higher

Anthropomorphic: A benefactor

Favorably Placed

Inheritance, bequest, donation, presents, raise in pay, unexpected windfall, charitable contribution, endowment, good luck, winnings, a service received or freely given, an offering of assistance

Unfavorably Placed

Duty, obligation, involuntary sacrifice, responsibility, dependants, toll, debt, burdens, required donations or observances, payments, evil consequences of a charitable act

Key: Sacrifice

 ## Wunjo: Glory

Joy or glory that stems from voluntary offerings. The fruits of sacrifice, which on a spiritual level are ecstasy, and on a temporal level, power.

Literal: Glory

Symbolic: Spiritual exaltation

Anthropomorphic: A hero

Favorably Placed

Victory, achievement, a prize, honors, dignities, celebrity, recognition of accomplishments, exultation, ecstasy, bliss, a divine reward, transcendence, personal well-being

Unfavorably Placed

Intoxication, delirium, wild enthusiasm, unrealistic plans, delusions of grandeur, excessive hopes or expectations, spirit possession, monomania, dreams of glory

Key: Happiness

 ## Hagalaz: Hail

The violent, destructive force of nature that beats down crops, kills livestock, and destroys homes. It comes without warning from the sky and strikes at random the just and unjust alike.

Literal: Hailstorm

Symbolic: Blind force of nature

Anthropomorphic: A destructive person

Favorably Placed

Triumph over adversity, strengthen through hardship, trial weathered, testing of metal, character building, turning failure into success, disaster narrowly averted, need to rebuild

Unfavorably Placed

Storm, destruction, natural violence, accident, wreck, injury by mishap, crime of passion, impulsive attack, injury by an animal, loss of possessions, material hardship

> *Key:* Hardship

 ## Nauthiz: Need

The necessity to endure hardship and suffering that cannot be avoided or overcome. There is no glory or victory in this endurance, only the dogged will to survive.

Literal: Suffering

Symbolic: Dark night of the soul

Anthropomorphic: A needy person

Favorably Placed

Endurance, stubborn will to resist, refusal to surrender, defiance of fate, escape from death, recovery from a long illness, tenacity, toughness, suffering overcome

Unfavorably Placed

Need, want, dire extremity, emotional or physical deprivation, loss of human dignity, suffering beyond the will to resist, failure of hope, emotional numbness, clinging to life, nakedness of the soul, starvation, exposure to the elements, torment, tortures of hell

> *Key:* Necessity

 ## Isa: Ice

The ice of winter that locks the growing things of the earth and the deep secret things of the sea beneath its glittering mirror. Ice allures the hapless traveler onto its easy surface and then fails under his feet.

Literal: Ice

Symbolic: Mask

Anthropomorphic: A deceiver

Favorably Placed

Glamour, infatuation, dreams of glory, glittering prizes, elusive desires, superficial beauty, beguiling words, illusions, seduction, obsessive love

Unfavorably Placed

Deceit, betrayal, hidden purpose, lies, manipulation, hindering, hurtful secrets, concealed meaning, plot, ambush, unforeseen disaster, cunning, stealth

> *Key:* Entrapment

 ## Jera: Harvest Season

Year, but more specifically the fulfillment of the year when the fruits of the summer are gathered in. The coming full circle or turning of the wheel of the seasons.

Literal: Harvest

Symbolic: Inversion

Anthropomorphic: A revolutionary

Favorably Placed

Conditions improve, transformation, alteration, fruition, things come together, upward cycle, waiting is over, fulfillment of labor, sea change, reassessment of situation

Unfavorably Placed

Setback, disappointment, small return on investment, state of confusion, hopes dashed, demotion, humbling experience, bitter harvest, reaping the whirlwind, anarchy, downward cycle

> *Key:* Change

 ## Eihwaz: Yew

The elastic, serviceable wood of the yew was used to make weapons of war, and also magical amulets of protection. The yew frequently grows in graveyards and is associated with spirits of the dead, perhaps having a protective or aversive function against the restless wandering of ghosts.

Literal: Yew tree

Symbolic: Reliability

Anthropomorphic: A dependable ally

Favorably Placed

Faithfulness, reliability, strength of purpose, the keeping of promises, fulfillment of responsibility, one who can be trusted, instrument that will not fail in use, something to depend upon, an honest servant, fidelity, magical weapon

Unfavorably Placed

Blind obedience, misplaced loyalty, lack of initiative, dullness, no imagination, meek bowing to circumstances, inability to assume authority, subservience, adherence to outmoded forms, inflexibility, too literal following of orders

    Key: Duty

Perth: Apple

The apple tree, its wood and fruit. The luscious apple is a universal symbol of luxury and indulgence in sensual pleasures.

Literal: Fruit of the apple

Symbolic: Forbidden delights

Anthropomorphic: A seducer

Favorably Placed

Abundance, opulence, satisfaction, enjoyment, celebration, indulgence, entertainment, sensuality, socializing, parties, games of chance, lovemaking

Unfavorably Placed

Excess, satiety, surfeit, revulsion, too much of a good thing, drunkenness, lust, perverse sexuality, decadence, illicit thrills, drug addiction, gluttony, rottenness, decay

    Key: Pleasure

Algiz: Defense

A warning sign for warding off under threat of painful consequences that may originate with the splayed human hand, or as seems to me more likely, with the talons of the hawk. It was carried into battle as an amulet of protection.

Literal: Warning

Symbolic: Taboo

Anthropomorphic: A guardian

Favorably Placed

Shield, protection, good angel, guardian spirit, defender, repulsion of evil, aid in battle, frustration of the foe, watchfulness, care, timely intervention, unbreachable defense

Unfavorably Placed

Danger, warning, what must be shunned, holding at arm's length, the forbidden, fatal attraction, inadequate defense, hidden threat, ostracized, scapegoat

> *Key:* Protection

 ## Sowelu: Sun

The Sun with its fiery rays that strike the earth like hammer blows to scorch and blast, but also the source of all heat and light and the giver of vitality.

Literal: The Sun

Symbolic: Spiritual fire

Anthropomorphic: An executioner of judgments

Favorably Placed

Bold action, initiative, the masterstroke, moving power, vital force, galvanizer, shattering of conceit, breaking the status quo, destroyer of inertia, decision, act of will, cutting red tape, striking to the heart, justice executed

Unfavorably Placed

Nemesis, retribution, an eye for an eye, punishment for sins, paying for past mistakes, exposure of guilt, divine thunderbolt, wrath of God, skeletons fall out of the closet, vengeance, blood feud, reprisal, pitiless calling to account

> *Key:* Judgment

 ## Teiwaz: Courage

The god after whom Tuesday receives it name. Originally a deity of oaths and legal contracts, in later times he became a war god renowned for his courage and honor. Warriors carried this rune into battle to heighten their valor.

Literal: God of war

Symbolic: Honor

Anthropomorphic: An honest arbitrator

Favorably Placed

Legal matters, court actions, settlements, judgments, affairs of honor, valor, heroism, eloquent defense, persuasion, witnesses come forth, fair dealing, equitable arrangement, truth upheld

Unfavorably Placed

Legal battles, protracted dispute, trickery, conflict, refusal to compromise, rejection of arbitration, delayed judgment, warfare, strife, arrogance, intolerance, clash of wills, attempt to dominate

Key: Judgment

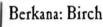 Berkana: Birch

The birch is the earliest tree to bud and turn green in the spring, and for this reason was used to promote fertility in livestock and in human beings. This belief is still honored when those who take saunas lash each other with birch twigs, on the pretext of stimulating the circulation.

Literal: The birch tree

Symbolic: Sexuality

Anthropomorphic: A pregnant woman

Favorably Placed

Fertility, desire, lovemaking, conception, creation, flow of ideas, beginning of growth, new project, inception, vital energy, rites of spring, sowing wild oats, first love, playfulness, cheer, initiation

Unfavorably Placed

Passion, abandon, obsession with youth, imprudence, dangerous infatuation, uncontrolled growth, possible cancer, risk of unwanted pregnancy, sexual disease, wantonness

Key: Fertility

Ehwaz: Horse

The necessary beast for travel over land and for making war, embodying in itself the essence of speed, power and beauty. Horses were worshipped as messengers of the gods by the Teutons.

Literal: Horse

Symbolic: The physical virtues

Anthropomorphic: An agent for someone else

Favorably Placed

Rapid progress, the means of transportation, medium of action, ability to leap over obstacles, advancement, grace, movement on any level, social climbing, promotion, any personal vehicle such as a car, boat, or private plane

Unfavorably Placed

Haste, recklessness, blind precipitation, heedlessness, a fool rushing in, fall over a precipice, forcing the issue, tempting fate, hurried business transaction, lack of control, intoxication with speed, racing, caution thrown to the wind, and imprudent purchase

Key: Conveyance

 ## Mannaz: Man

The primordial man, Adam, who is the archetype of the human race, called by the ancient Germans Mannus. He represents the highest powers of the human mind, those qualities that separate humanity from the beasts.

Literal: First man

Symbolic: The mental virtues

Anthropomorphic: A magician

Favorably Placed

Intelligence, foresight, vision, creative thought, craftsmanship, invention, insight, logic, skill, ideas, plans, patterns, design, analysis, clear expression of purpose

Unfavorably Placed

Cunning, craftiness, calculation, slyness, misdirection, slight of hand, deception, manipulation, fraud, con artist, trickster, illusionist, shape-changer, the wearer of masks, lies, machinations

    Key: Intelligence

Laguz: Water

Water in all of its bewildering variety of forms, from the salt waves of the sea to the rushing power of a mighty river to the clear coolness of a forest spring, including the hidden depths of the unconscious mind.

Literal: Water

Symbolic: Imagination

Anthropomorphic: A medium or psychic

Favorably Placed

A body of water, the ocean, changeableness, adaptability, receptiveness, emotions, sentimentality, romantics, dreamers, poets, musicians, artistic expression, imagination, fantasies, mysteries, mediumship, the occult

Unfavorably Placed

Madness, obsession, mania, melancholy, nightmares, the hidden, the submerged, deep dark secrets, the underworld, suppressed thoughts and impulses, depression, suicide, drugs, escapism, excessive sleep, catatonia, coma

    Key: Unconscious

Inguz: Fertility God

Ing is the name of a god of the Danes who presided over the family hearth and the productive growth of the fields. Whereas Berkana rules the conception of life, Inguz rules its fulfillment.

Literal: God of the earth

Symbolic: Fruitfulness

Anthropomorphic: A father or mother

Favorably Placed

The patriarch, head of the house, the home, family, simple virtues, honest work, common sense, increase in value, stability, continuity, nurturing environment, growth of children, productive employment, human warmth, love

Unfavorably Placed

Toil, drudgery, domestic enslavement, family responsibilities, stress, worry about career, dissatisfaction, obsession with improving lifestyle, social climbing, pressure upon children to achieve, concern about the home, budget worries, renovations to the house

Key: Growth

 ## Dagaz: Day

The light of the Sun and the period of its cycle around the earth, with the associations of reason, order, and completeness.

Literal: Daylight

Symbolic: Perfection

Anthropomorphic: A teacher

Favorably Placed

Clarity, total view, shadows dispelled, answer revealed, all facts known, tying up loose ends, fulfillment of cycle, coming full circle, period of study or labor, phase of life, lifespan, end meeting the beginning, unit of time, reincarnation

Unfavorably Placed

End of growth, finish of career, breakup of a relationship, end of the road, future uncertain, limitation, boundary, termination, enclosure, fence, wall, prison, lengthening shadows, fear of the unknown, step into darkness, death

Key: Completion

Othila: Homeland

The hereditary possession of a people, which can be as simple as a plot of land or a house, or as extensive as a vast nation that has endured for centuries.

Literal: Native land

Symbolic: What defines identity

Anthropomorphic: An ancestor

Favorably Placed

Land, deed, property, house, region of birth, native country, where the heart is, accomplishments in life, inherited talents, acquired skills, credentials, works, what has been carved out by trial or won by valor, citizenship, passport, patriotism, pride of race

Unfavorably Placed

Inhospitality, homelessness, wandering, exile, loss of property, loss of passport or citizenship, lack of roots, bad habits, accumulated vices, haunting memories, prejudices, bigotry, provincial attitudes, insularity, class consciousness, clannishness, jingoism, isolationism, protectionism, the grave

Key: Home

6

The Zodiac Signs

The twelve signs of the zodiac take their inspiration from and are loosely related to twelve ancient constellations of stars that bear the same names. The placement of the signs does not correspond exactly with the location of the physical constellations. Each sign occupies and influences an even 30 degrees of the circle of the chart, and relates by its inherent identity to one of the twelve houses.

The signs express the basic types of human nature, and by extension the way these differing psychological types act and react in the world. The signs are the modes of expression through which the life principles or active energies of the planets flow.

Abstractly, each sign is compounded from the united workings of one of the three qualities and one of the four elements. These two sets divide the zodiac into three groups of four signs, and four groups of three signs, indicated on the following diagrams respectively by squares and triangles:

Figure 6-1

Quadruplicities

Cardinal: Aries, Cancer, Libra, Capricorn

Fixed: Leo, Scorpio, Aquarius, Taurus

Mutable: Sagittarius, Pisces, Gemini, Virgo

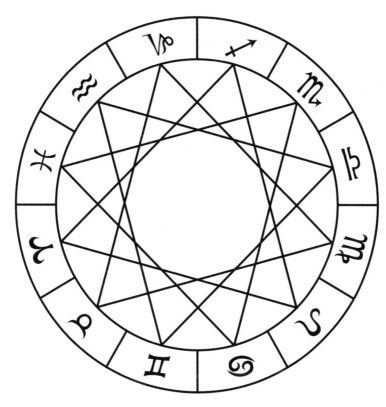

Figure 6-2

Triplicities

Fire: Aries, Leo, Sagittarius

Water: Cancer, Scorpio, Pisces

Air: Libra, Aquarius, Gemini

Earth: Capricorn, Taurus, Virgo

Another even more fundamental pattern in the signs is the alternation of positive and negative, or male and female, signs beginning with male Aries. Generally speaking, positive signs are more active and spontaneous, while negative signs tend to be passive and repressed in their working. Notice that the triplicities of fire and air are all positive signs, while the water and Earth triplicities are all negative.

Aries

Symbol: The Ram

Glyph: ♈

Ruler: Mars

House: 1st

Polarity: Positive

Class: Cardinal fire

Part of Body: Head

Type: Aggressive, impulsive, courageous, assertive, enterprising, passionate, quick-witted, hot-tempered, restless, forceful, *but also* bullying, rude, insensitive, impatient, foolhardy

Role: Leader, explorer, sportsman or sportswoman, engineer, soldier, surgeon, positions of initiative

Instruments: Sword, knife, cutting edge

Key: Urgency

Taurus

Symbol: The Bull

Glyph: ♉

Ruler: Venus

House: 2nd

Polarity: Negative

Class: Fixed earth

Parts of Body: Throat, neck, and shoulders

Type: Reliable, careful, practical, steadfast, methodical, productive, sensual, patient, enduring, *but also* possessive, stubborn, obstinate, dull, self-repressed, unimaginative

Role: Builder, economist, civil servant, accountant, farm worker, craftsman, manager, singer, jeweller, banker

Instruments: Earth, clay, stone, products of the soil

Key: Perseverance

Gemini

Symbol: The Twins

Glyph: ♊

Ruler: Mercury

House: 3rd

Polarity: Positive

Class: Mutable air

Parts of Body: Hands, arms, and lungs

Type: Versatile, adaptive, talkative, intelligent, ingenious, witty, social, inquisitive, agile, *but also* superficial, inconsistent, cunning, nervous

Role: Writer, teacher, lecturer, agent, publicist, mediator, reporter, salesman, travel guide, secretary, lawyer

Instruments: Pen, computer

Key: Communication

Cancer

Symbol: The Crab

Glyph: ♋

Ruler: Moon

House: 4th

Polarity: Negative

Class: Cardinal water

Parts of Body: Breast, ovaries, womb, stomach

Type: Sensitive, impressionable, loyal, patriotic, emotional, imaginative, home-loving, tender, protective, *but also* clannish, acquisitive, moody, retentive, clinging, fussy, crabby, defensive, reserved, timid, self-pitying

Role: Nurse, trustee, flight attendant, architectural or artistic restorer, librarian, house-keeper, antique dealer, hotel operator, bartender, positions of keeping and protecting

Instruments: Net, noose, lock

Key: Protection

Leo

Symbol: The Lion

Glyph: ♌

Ruler: Sun

House: 5th

Polarity: Positive

Class: Fixed fire

Parts of Body: Heart, spine

Type: Dignified, self-assured, commanding, powerful, generous, reliable, magnanimous, faithful, noble, warm-hearted, outgoing, *but also* intolerant, conceited, pompous, self-assured, domineering, snobbish, patronizing, autocratic

Role: Leader, organizer, director, chairperson, boss, military officer, manager, actor

Instruments: Scepter, baton, gold pen (signature)

Key: Authority

Virgo

Symbol: The Virgin

Glyph: ♍

Ruler: Mercury

House: 6th

Polarity: Negative

Class: Mutable earth

Parts of Body: Intestines, nervous system

Type: Analytical, critical, methodical, discerning, precise, intelligent, conscientious, clean, modest, *but also* fastidious, reserved, stand-offish, suppressed, hypocritical, neat-freak, hypochondriac, pedantic, fault-finding, irritable, resentful

Role: Health care, sanitation, environmental protection, inspector, dietitian, craftsman, grower, doctor, critic, teacher, charity or social worker, skilled laborer, plumber, bricklayer, psychiatrist

Instruments: Cleaning implements, measuring devices

Key: Analysis

Libra

Symbol: The Scales

Glyph: ♎

Ruler: Venus

House: 7th

Polarity: Positive

Class: Cardinal air

Parts of Body: Kidneys, lower back

Type: Charming, diplomatic, outgoing, fashion-conscious, gregarious, kind, easygoing, cooperative, romantic, *but also* indolent, indecisive, shallow, soft, untidy, discontented, vacillating, weak, depressed, lazy

Role: Artist, diplomat, mediator, host, hairstylist, clothing designer, poet, public speaker

Instruments: Clothing, jewelry, cosmetics

Key: Harmony

Scorpio

Symbol: The Scorpion

Glyph: ♏

Ruler: Mars

House: 8th

Polarity: Negative

Class: Fixed water

Parts of Body: Sex organs

Type: Passionate, deep, mystical, erotic, magnetic, subtle, purposeful, penetrating, *but also* secretive, jealous, stubborn, resentful, suspicious, vindictive, destructive, vicious, cruel, calculating

Role: Surgeon, soldier, butcher, marine, police detective, scientist, psychologist, mortician, psychic investigator, mystic, healer

Instruments: Needle, probe, scalpel, gun

Key: Penetration

Sagittarius

Symbol: The Horse-archer

Glyph: ♐

Ruler: Jupiter

House: 9th

Polarity: Positive

Class: Mutable fire

Parts of Body: Hips and thighs

Type: Intellectual, ambitious, restless, forward-looking, curious, energetic, active, playful, daring, *but also* boastful, careless, boisterous, extravagant, selfish, temperamental, uncontrolled, extreme, tactless

Role: Explorer, philosopher, athlete, coach, animal trainer, show-jumper or jockey, interpreter, translator, lawmaker, hunter, publisher

Instruments: Bow, whip, spurs, bridle

Key: Exploration

Capricorn

Symbol: The Goat

Glyph: ♑

Ruler: Saturn

House: 10th

Polarity: Negative

Class: Cardinal earth

Parts of Body: Knees, bones, skin

Type: Responsible, practical, hardworking, ambitious, prudent, disciplined, persevering, methodical, resourceful, enduring, cautious, *but also* calculating, severe, unfeeling, selfish, miserly, cruel, pessimistic, narrow-minded, worrying, negative

Role: Politician, builder, engineer, mathematician, stockbroker, manager, civil servant, lab technician, pharmacist

Instruments: Grindstone, mortar and pestle, slide rule

Key: Discipline

Aquarius

Symbol: The Water-bearer

Glyph: ≈

Ruler: Saturn

House: 11th

Polarity: Positive

Class: Fixed air

Parts of Body: Shin and ankle

Type: Original, idealistic, thoughtful, intuitive, expressive, communicative, inventive, progressive, independent, *but also* impersonal, detached, opinionated, fanatical, rebellious, rude, intolerant, impatient, cranky, isolated, malcontent, eccentric

Role: Photographer, astronomer, radiologist, newscaster, archaeologist, electrical engineer, astrologer, physicist, social reformer

Instruments: Camera, television, radio

Key: Reformation

Pisces

Symbol: The Fishes

Glyph: ♓

Ruler: Jupiter

House: 12th

Polarity: Negative

Class: Mutable water

Part of Body: Feet

Type: Emotional, impressionable, receptive, intuitive, submissive, loving, sensitive, self-sacrificing, devoted, nurturing, *but also* impractical, dependent, gullible, vague, unfocused, confused, malleable, extravagant, variable, careless, escapist, dreaming

Role: Spirit medium, psychic, artist, actor, dancer, priest, veterinarian, fisherman or fisherwoman, romance novelist, songwriter, anesthetist

Instruments: Veils, sails, colored glasses

Key: Reception

The Houses

The houses of astrology are twelve temporal divisions of the ecliptic—the apparent path of the Sun across the heavens. The ecliptic lies within the zodiac, an imaginary band that extends nine degrees above and nine degrees below the ecliptic. The houses are closely related to the signs, which divide the zodiac into twelve parts. The Ascendant is the degree of the zodiac rising above the eastern horizon at the given moment for which a chart is cast. It always marks the first degree of the 1st house, and it is through the Ascendant that the ring of the signs is oriented in relation to the concentric ring of the houses. If the Ascendant happens to fall on the first degree of Aries, the signs will occupy their "natural" houses, the houses with which they are in the greatest accord. This rarely occurs. Usually, the houses are rotated upon the ring of signs out of their natural placements.

On the standard chart of conventional astrology, the 1st house is always located on the left side of the zodiac below the Ascendant degree, which begins it. The signs are written in later based upon the location of the Ascendant in a particular sign at the moment for which the horoscope is cast. The Ascendant moves in a complete circle through the twelve signs once each day, just as the Sun appears to move around the heavens in the same period.

On the runic astrology chart, the position of the signs is nominally fixed, and the rotation of the ring of the houses varies with the location of the Ascendant. This was done because the runes are linked to the signs, and it would have been too much work to draw in all the runes each time a chart was erected if it were necessary to enter the signs upon the small chart rather than the houses.

If you think about it, you will see that the end result is exactly the same. Whether you fix the ring of the signs and rotate the ring of the houses, or fix the ring of the houses and rotate the ring of the signs, the relationship between the houses and signs will be identical because the same locator—the position of the Ascendant in the zodiac—is used in both cases.

If you are used to reading the standard astrological chart, you may want to turn the runic astrology chart until the Ascendant is positioned on the middle left. Then the runic astrology chart can be read in the same manner as a regular astrology chart. After some familiarity is gained with the variably placed Ascendant, this will probably no longer be necessary.

The meaning of the twelve houses is the murkiest question in modern astrology. The reason for this is simple. Centuries ago astrologers did not make a clear distinction between the houses and signs. For example, the meaning of the third sign, Gemini, and the 3rd house, called the Goddess, was essentially the same. As astrology progressed, the signs and houses began to be differentiated, but the houses continue even in the present to draw their meanings from their related signs. Astrologers seeking to distinguish between houses and signs are inhibited by the fact that, at root, they have the same meanings.

Nonetheless, it is possible to draw a distinction. The root meanings of the signs and houses may be the same, but the interpretation of the signs, due to the dynamic nature of the zodiac, is different from the interpretation of the houses, which is based upon their static, or fixed, natures.

The houses are essentially time divisions. They may be thought of as a grid, or underlying framework, upon which all the other elements of the chart are related and interpreted. The houses are tied to the rotation of the Earth upon its axis, as is the Ascendant, their locator in relation to the heavens. It will greatly aid the understanding if the zodiac signs are regarded as heavenly, and the houses as earthly.

Conceive the houses as a background (a setting, or environment, or spheres of life) upon which the active environmental forces of the signs operate. The essential meaning is the same, but the interpretation is different, just as the word "flower" can be interpreted differently when used as a noun or a verb, even though it concerns the same underlying concept.

This distinction has led to the houses being described as material interests and conditions, and the signs as spiritual qualities and temperaments.[1] The signs, regarded as active, are associated with life and the spirit; the houses, regarded as the static background, are associated with the material and the manifest. The signs represent the manner or way of action, the houses the kind of activity or matter acted upon or interacted with. Perhaps it is best to think of the houses as the manifesting sphere for the power of the signs.

As was mentioned earlier, runic astrology uses an ideal, or symbolic, system of astrology that is not bound by the actual physical variations of the heavens. In fact, all astrology is ideal to a greater or a lesser extent, but runic astrology does not even pay lip service to changing astronomical conditions. The house system used here is the system of equal houses. All houses are exactly 30 degrees of arc, just as all signs are 30 degrees. This greatly simplifies the erection and reading of the chart, but it should not be assumed that meaning is lost as a result of this simplicity. Many of the finest modern astrologers, including Jeff Mayo, use an equal house division.[2] Since runic astrology is not in any way tied to the actual positions of the planets in the sky, an equal house system is the best choice.

The first six houses are said to be personal, because in their natural positions they occupy the dark hemisphere that lies beneath the line of the horizon and so signify what is hidden and internal. The last six houses are said to be interpersonal, because they occupy the light hemisphere above the horizon and so signify what is manifest and external.

First House

Name: The Horoscope

Glyph: I or 1st

Natural Sign: Aries

The 1st house is named the Horoscope, from the Greek for "time observer." It receives this name because it establishes through the Ascendant in its first degree the entire structure of the chart. The name "Ascendant" is also applied to the 1st house as a whole. This house refers to the matter or question with which the divination is concerned. If it is a life reading, it relates to the querent. Much can be learned about the physical and mental qualities of the querent from the planets that occupy the Ascendant house. It also reveals personal interests or fixations that define and establish separateness—what distinguishes an individual from others.

In understanding this house, consideration must be given to the sign Aries and the planet Mars, both of which strongly influence its nature.

Key: Self-interest

Second House

Name: Gate of Hades

Glyph: II or 2nd

Natural Sign: Taurus

The 2nd house refers to personal possessions and emotions, possessiveness, the accumulation of wealth, and the attainment of financial and material security. Matters of business, estate arrangements, and relations acquired through marriage all pertain to the 2nd house. It also concerns the body and the senses, the response of the individual to tastes, scents, colors, sounds, and textures.

In understanding this house, consideration must be given to the nature of the sign Taurus and the planet Venus.

Key: Possession

Third House

Name: The Goddess

Glyph: III or 3rd

Natural Sign: Gemini

The goddess to which the name of this house refers is the Moon. The 3rd house concerns communication in all its forms, verbal, written, and visual. Letters, lectures, telegrams, phone calls, speeches, and instructions all fall into the sphere of this house. It also pertains, through the influence of Mercury, to the need to relate with others and integrate with the immediate surroundings. Close family relations, especially brothers and sisters, are connected with this house. It has to do with activity of a superficial social type, such as visiting, vacationing, and celebrating, as well as similar shallow mental activities such as gossip and casual party chatter.

In understanding this house, consideration must be given to the nature of the sign Gemini and the planet Mercury.

Key: Inter-relationship

Fourth House

Name: Lower Midheaven

Glyph: IV or 4th

Natural Sign: Cancer

The 4th house relates to the home and hearth and, therefore, to the parents, hereditary property, and place of residence. This house has to do with the start and end of life, childhood, and the grave. It may also refer to occult matters and things of the unconscious.

In understanding this house, consideration must be given to the nature of the sign Cancer and the Moon.

Key: Home ground

Fifth House

Name: The Good Fortune

Glyph: V or 5th

Natural Sign: Leo

The 5th house concerns creative and expansive activities that contribute to pleasure and a joy in living. One form of this creative activity is the creation of offspring, and children fall into the sphere of this house. Also games, sports, speculation and gambling, as well as lovemaking as a sportive activity. Writing, acting, painting, and other expressive acts may show their influence here.

In understanding this house, consideration must be given to the nature of the sign Leo and the Sun.

Key: Self-expression

Sixth House

Name: The Bad Fortune

Glyph: VI or 6th

Natural Sign: Virgo

The 6th house concerns practical labor, efficiency, a sense of duty and service to the community, especially in the fields of health and hygiene in employments such as nursing, sanitation, architectural renovation, and public works. The physical health and cleanliness of the individual, and any possible sickness, are also revealed by this house, which is connected with body-mind wholeness and holistic healing.

In understanding this house, consideration must be given to the nature of the sign Virgo and the planet Mercury.

Key: Service

Seventh House

Name: The Occident

Glyph: VII or 7th

Natural Sign: Libra

The 7th house is named the Occident because it is located at the Descendant in the west. It concerns the formation of close relations and ties with others such as marriages, business partnerships, love unions, friendships, and balanced unions of mutual dependence. These relationships are not necessarily harmonious, and may even be destructive, but they always involve equal need in both parties.

In understanding this house, consideration must be given to the nature of the sign Libra and the planet Venus.

Key: Partnership

Eighth House

Name: The Beginning of Death

Glyph: VIII or 8th

Natural Sign: Scorpio

The 8th house concerns the material dependence of one person upon another, or others, and the sharing of possessions and personal resources such as time and labor, self-sacrifice, and possible spiritual rebirth. This is a house of strong passions and feelings. It has traditionally been closely linked with death, and it may refer to the exchange of money, estates, or other possessions through legacies and wills, death benefits, and insurance payments.

In understanding this house, consideration must be given to the nature of the sign Scorpio and the planet Mars.

Key: Self-sacrifice

Ninth House

Name: The God

Glyph: IX or 9th

Natural Sign: Sagittarius

The deity referred to in the name of the 9th house is the Sun. It is the house of profound mental activity and extended travel, communications that are protracted and significant such as serious studies in higher education or in training for a professional career, university education away from the home, study of foreign languages, and places distant in time and space. It is also linked to dreams and prophecy, and may generally be said to involve the extension of awareness beyond the everyday sphere of living.

In understanding this house, consideration must be given to the nature of the sign Sagittarius and the planet Jupiter.

Key: Personal growth

Tenth House

Name: Midheaven

Glyph: X or 10th

Natural Sign: Capricorn

The 10th house is named Midheaven because it is located at the high point on the circle of the heavens. It is the house concerned with the outward expression of the self in daily living and the attainment of career or life goals. Social status, position in the community, personal ambitions, and the quest for material success all fall into the sphere of this house. It relates to interests of a practical nature that exist beyond the immediate circle of home and family—establishing a place in the world.

In understanding this house, consideration must be given to the nature of the sign Capricorn and the planet Saturn.

Key: Career

Eleventh House

Name: The Good Daemon

Glyph: XI or 11th

Natural Sign: Aquarius

The 11th house is named the Good Daemon, which is the angel said to stand at the right shoulder of every person and constantly encourage good thoughts. This house concerns group activities, social causes, political and reformist movements that involve social bonds and shared purposes, including clubs, societies, and camaraderie. This is the house of wishes and hopes and all life objectives formed by circumstances that change with the changing conditions of a life. Interests, diversions, hobbies, causes, and commitments to ideas.

In understanding this house, consideration must be given to the nature of the sign Aquarius and the planet Saturn.

Key: Group activity

Twelfth House

Name: The Bad Daemon

Glyph: XII or 12th

Natural Sign: Pisces

The 12th house is called the Bad Daemon, equivalent to the dark angel said to stand at the left shoulder of every person and whisper evil suggestions. It is also referred to as the house of sorrows. It concerns enemies, the end of life, secret sacrifices, long unrewarded service, confinement, sickness, and mental illness. Hospitals, prisons, monasteries and nunneries, asylums, and other confining, detached places of group residence fall into the sphere of this house, which is also connected with psychic activity, intuition, mediumship, and the unconscious mind. All thankless labor and sacrifice for others belongs here.

In understanding this house, consideration must be given to the nature of the sign Pisces and the planet Jupiter.

Key: Selflessness

8

The Planets

In ancient times the planets were known as the seven wandering bodies, so called because they moved in complex ways against the seemingly changeless backdrop of the fixed stars. They consisted of five points of light of various colors, known as Mercury, Venus, Mars, Jupiter, and Saturn, and two orbs, the Sun and the Moon. No other planets were known to exist, nor was it realized that the five points of light that wander through the heavens are actually material masses of roughly spherical shape. It is important to realize these things if we are to see the planets the way the early astrologers saw them.

Runic astrology uses only the seven planets of traditional astrology, which are related to the twelve signs of the zodiac in an elegant bilateral symmetry on either side of an imaginary axis that runs between Moon-ruled Cancer and Sun-ruled Leo. On either side of the signs of the Moon and Sun, the five planets that show points of light are arranged in two sets of opposite pairs extending away in their traditional order from quickest to slowest apparent motion, as observed from Earth. Each of the seven planets occupies the sign or signs it is said to rule. The Sun and Moon rule only one sign each, but the other planets rule two signs each. Planets have a strong natural accord with the signs they dominate.

The planets are the focal points for the active drives or urges of the unconscious, and represent basic principles of life energy. It is the placement of each planet that draws the attention to a particular point on the concentric rings of the heavenly signs and earthly houses, and causes that point to be considered in relation to other points, also located by planets. For this reason the planets have been called "catalytic agents,"[1] a description that may be misleading, since a catalyst is a material that promotes a chemical reaction without

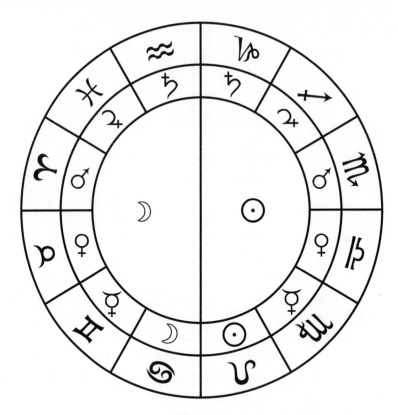

Figure 8-1

itself being a part of that reaction, whereas the planets are very definitely a part of the interpretation of the astrological chart.

Each planet is composed of one, two, or three simple qualities, which are represented
in astrology by the glyphs of the circle, crescent, and cross, relating respectively to the Sun,
Moon, and Earth. The five planets that appear only as points of light are compounds of
these qualities in various relationships, with one quality dominant over the other, or others.
Mercury is the only classical planet made up of all three simple qualities, as reflected in its
glyph of three parts. The glyph of the Moon is essentially a simple crescent, or half circle,
revealing its pure, unmixed nature. The glyph of Venus, on the other hand, is compounded
of a simple circle, representing the quality of the Sun, set over the cross, representing the

quality of earth. An analysis of these symbol-elements in the planetary glyphs, and their inter-relationships, will give a clear and full comprehension of the planets.

The occult correspondences given below for each of the planets are the traditional correspondences:

Planet	Glyph	Metal	Color	Number	Body-part
Moon	☽	Silver	Silvery	9	Breasts, womb
Mercury	☿	Mercury	Orange	8	Lungs, throat
Venus	♀	Copper	Green	7	Lower back, kidneys, veins, throat
Sun	☉	Gold	Golden	6	Heart
Mars	♂	Iron	Red	5	Head, penis, testicles
Jupiter	♃	Tin	Blue	4	Liver, hips, thighs
Saturn	♄	Lead	Black	3	Lower legs, bones

Moon

The source of rhythmic change manifesting in such things as the tides, the menses, and mood swings. The Moon commands the emotions and desires, habits of behavior, and instinctive responses. It stands at the gateway between the past and the present, and between the everyday reality and the hidden, underlying nature of things. The Moon represents the unconscious mind, dreams, visions, and spirit communication.

Glyph: ☽

Color: Silvery

Metal: Silver

Number: 9

Polarity: Female

Sign: Cancer

Principle: Rhythm, instinct, response, assimilation, reflection, evolution, duality, organic growth, motherhood, femininity, emotionalism, mental instability, reflexes, habits, affection, desire, moods, memory, the past, the unconscious, dreams, visions, mediumship, restlessness, changeability, deep associations, mother complex

Type: Changeable, retentive, imaginative, maternal, protective, receptive, sensitive, tenacious, *but also* irrational, fussy, indrawn, susceptible, touchy, unreliable, resentful, withholding

Role: Psychic, spirit medium, romantic, pediatrician, day-care worker, sailor, fisherman, fisherwoman, matriarch

Key: Rhythmic response

Mercury

This is the only traditional planet that balances in itself the three simple qualities of Sun, Moon, and Earth. For this reason it is feminine and lunar with the Moon, but masculine and solar with the Sun. Mercury is often said to have no nature of its own, but this chameleon talent is itself a legitimate and distinct life principle. Mercury is associated with all communication by thought and words, eloquence, and learning, as well as all forms of travel. It represents the intellect, writings, diplomacy, cunning speech and actions, and the science of medicine.

Glyph: ☿

Color: Orange

Metal: Mercury

Number: 8

Polarity: Androgynous

Signs: Gemini and Virgo

Principle: Communication, coordination, transmission, mind, reason, logic, eloquence, cunning, craft, commerce, nervous energy, integration, interpretation, analysis, transformation, development, instruction, expression, adjustment, interaction

Type: Clever, cool, unemotional, logical, adept, deft, expressive, perceptive, precise, versatile, talkative, apt, adroit, inquisitive, *but also* sly, nervous, chattering, diffuse, critical, superficial, slick, artful, shallow, nosy, gossipy, fault-finding

Role: Messenger, mediator, coordinator, manager, actor, reporter, narrator, tour guide, public speaker, entertainer, agent, middleman, salesman

Key: Communication

Venus

Venus is composed of the solar quality, expressed in its glyph by the circle, acting upon the foundation of the earthy quality expressed by the cross. It represents the feminine in both sexes—the glyph of Venus is used as the symbol for woman. Emotion, sensitivity, empathy, and the impulse that unifies and harmonizes to resolve conflicts fall under the influence of Venus, which is linked with partnerships and close relationships.

Glyph: ♀

Color: Green

Metal: Copper

Number: 7

Polarity: Female

Signs: Taurus and Libra

Principle: Unity, sympathy, feeling, evaluation, feminine, love, beauty, birthing, production, amorous, eroticism, cohesion, inclusive formation, volatile, warmth, passive, steady, serenity, wholesome, subjective, receptive, soft, soothing, resolve, affection, artistry, estheticism, attraction, accumulating, good fortune

Type: Gentle, harmonious, graceful, tactful, loving, pacific, compassionate, adaptable, creative, placid, sympathetic, *but also* indecisive, indefinite, unsatisfied, languid, lazy, weak-willed, irritable, oversensitive, overly romantic, dilettante, clotheshorse

Role: Dancer, fashion designer, art critic, waiter, artist, gourmet cook, jewelry maker, interior decorator, wine seller

Key: Cooperation

Sun

The constant, unchanging source of warmth and light, the Sun is the most powerful factor in the horoscope. The Sun reveals the type of person with whom the reading is concerned. The Sun is said to represent the father, but, more broadly, it stands for the creative father of the universe. It is the active power of the spirit, the vitality, the self-expression, the essential self.

Glyph: ☉

Color: Golden

Metal: Gold

Number: 6

Polarity: Male

Sign: Leo

Principle: Self-integration, wholeness, completeness, divine spirit, creative power, masculine, fatherhood, deity, authority, governing force, energizing factor, vitality, self-expression

Type: Dignified, faithful, cheerful, regal, powerful, magnanimous, dominant, vital, affectionate, proud, playful, *but also* arrogant, despotic, pompous, overbearing, autocratic, childish, extravagant, profligate, condescending, domineering

Role: Leader, teacher, politician, guru, authority figure, patriarch

Key: Expression of self

Mars

Mars is composed of the earth quality, represented by the cross in its glyph (which has in modern times evolved into an arrowhead), exalted over the solar quality, represented by the circle—matter ruling spirit. It represents physical action, violent force, strong will, courage, quick and thoughtless passions, and powerful sexual drives. It stands for the masculine in both male and female, and the glyph is used as the symbol for man. Mars is not necessarily evil since courage and the will to triumph are needed in all walks of life.

Glyph: ♂

Color: Red

Metal: Iron

Number: 5

Polarity: Male

Signs: Aries and Scorpio

Principle: Activity, self-assertion, power, enterprise, forceful expression, sensuality, initiation, objectivity, masculinity, warfare, generation, passion, lust, sex, consummation, stimulation, aggression, resistance, self-preservation, elimination

Type: Constructive, courageous, pioneering, energetic, forceful, direct, quick, combative, impulsive, passionate, virile, sensual, *but also* aggressive, cruel, foolhardy, angry, destructive, impatient, restless, rude, blunt, thoughtless, lustful, pugnacious, combative, violent, belligerent

Role: Soldier, athlete, revolutionary, fighter, explorer, pioneer, adventurer, hunter, police, criminal

Key: Self-assertion

Jupiter

Jupiter is formed from the lunar quality of rhythm and the human soul, represented in its glyph by the crescent, exalted and ruling over the earthy cross of matter, represented by the cross. This indicates reason and understanding, with a regular controlled growth or expansion; also, a personal awareness firmly based upon practical experience. This planet represents the urge to expand the consciousness to attain an understanding and control over the personal world. It is related to law both secular and religious, justice, morality, ethics, and the social order.

Glyph: ♃

Color: Blue

Metal: Tin

Number: 4

Polarity: Male

Signs: Pisces and Sagittarius

Principle: Expansion, growth, comprehension, development, higher consciousness, justice, law, virtue, rulership, protection, healing, purification, understanding, maturing, conscience, compensation, mercy, joviality, preservation, order, morality

Type: Expansive, generous, sportive, fortunate, cheerful, optimistic, broad-minded, ethical, temperate, *but also* exaggerating, extravagant, conceited, procrastinating, extremist, imprudent, wasteful, provocative

Role: Judge, legislator, chairman, foreman, head, landlord, religious leader, commander, president, superintendent

Key: Expansion

Saturn

Saturn is formed of the earth quality, represented in its glyph by the cross, exalted over the lunar quality, expressed by the crescent—matter ruling the soul. This planet has a strong influence upon the body and indicates physical limits such as old age and death, as well as the disorder known as melancholia. This disease can take two forms that suggest the dual nature of Saturn: simple melancholy is a black, soul-destroying depression; divine melancholy is a madness of creative inspiration that often afflicts great philosophers and artists. Dense, slow Saturn occupies the highest of the traditional spheres of the planets, the one nearest the realm of deity, and this causes Saturn to be paradoxically both earthy and spiritual in nature.

Glyph: ♄

Color: Black

Metal: Lead

Number: 3

Polarity: Female

Signs: Aquarius and Capricorn

Principle: Restriction, discipline, rigidity, limitation, contraction, materialistic, binding, crystallized, constriction, congestion, cool, fixed, containing, defining, apportioning, measure, withhold, dryness, concentration, practical, realism, duty, construction, separation, isolation, fear, suffering, denial, inadequacy, inhibition, withdrawal, hardship, melancholy

Type: Cautious, prudent, just, patient, careful, serious, thrifty, practical, responsible, controlled, aspiring, *but also* depressed, dull, miserly, severe, dogmatic, fearful, selfish, cruel, barren, sickly, heartless

Role: Architect, builder, stone mason, brick layer, philosopher, contemplative monk or nun, recluse, computer programmer, theologian, archaeologist, librarian

Key: Limitation

9

The Angles and Nodes

The four angles and the two nodes of the Moon are not heavenly bodies, but describe significant points in space found upon the path traced by the apparent revolution of the Sun about the Earth, called the ecliptic. At various times the Sun occupies all six of these spatial points, as viewed from Earth, but it is not necessary for the Sun to be in them for the points to exist. It is important to emphasize this fact to forestall confusion.

The angles are created by the relationship between the Sun and the Earth; the nodes are created by the relationship between the Sun and the Moon.

The Angles

The four corners of the heavens that mark the positions of the Sun at sunrise, noon, sunset, and midnight are called the angles. In an ideal sense, they are considered to lie at right angles to each other, separated by 90 degrees, and define a cross through the center of the zodiac, bisecting it into arcs above and below the horizon, and arcs east and west of the meridian—an imaginary circle around the Earth that intersects the poles, and is located by the position of the Sun at noon.

Think of the Earth as a sphere, surrounded by the band of the zodiac in a way similar to that of the ring of dust that surrounds the planet Saturn. Standing on the surface of the Earth, if we could look up and see this band, it would arch across the sky like a great rainbow, rising in the east and descending in the west. It continues unbroken around the dark side of the Earth. The path traced by the Sun across the sky follows this band of the zodiac. The Sun at noon, when it reaches its highest point in the heavens, marks the division of this

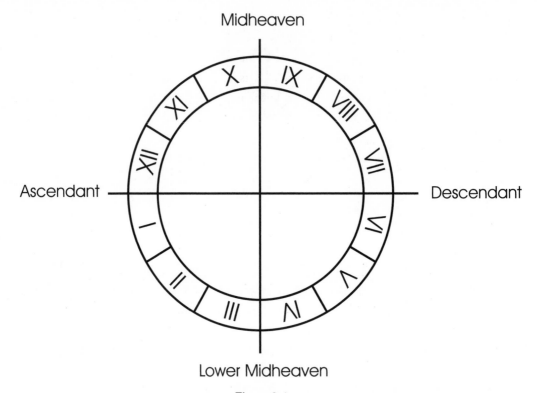

Figure 9-1

ring of the zodiac into its eastern semicircle and its western semicircle. In the same way, the horizon of the Earth marks the dividing line of the zodiac into a northern semicircle across the sky, and a southern semicircle that wraps underneath the Earth.

The Ascendant is the first degree of the 1st house (called the Horoscope); the Descendant is the first degree of the 7th house (called the Occident); the Midheaven is the first degree of the 10th house (called Midheaven); and the Lower Midheaven is the first degree of the 4th house (called Lower Midheaven).

The upper or southern arc of light (houses VII-XII) affects consciousness and objectivity; the lower or northern arc of darkness (houses I-VI) affects the unconscious and the subjective. The left or eastern arc of ascending and strengthening (houses X-III), affects the individual awareness, while the right or western arc of descending and weakening (houses IV-IX), affects the group awareness.

In an ideal sense, the Ascendant and Midheaven are at a right angle to each other, but in conventional astrology this seldom occurs. When a chart is drawn up, usually the angle is less or more than 90 degrees, depending upon the time of the year. However, since runic astrology does not refer to the actual positions of the planets in the heavens when casting a chart, Midheaven may be assumed to occupy its ideal location, at a perfect right angle to the Ascendant.

In what is called the quadrant house system of conventional astrology, the Midheaven degree is always located upon the cusp, or first degree, of the 10th house, regardless of the angle between the Midheaven and the Ascendant. This necessitates making some houses larger than 30 degrees and some smaller, in order to fit three houses into each quarter. The resulting distortion is inelegant and, in my opinion, unnecessary. Runic astrology uses an equal house system, in which all houses are presumed to be exactly 30 degrees.

Ascendant

The Ascendant is the point where the eastern horizon intersects the ecliptic. It is the place occupied by the Sun at the moment of sunrise, but it is not tied to the Sun. Think of it as the degree on the great circle of the ecliptic that is just rising above the eastern horizon at any given moment.

It is the Ascendant that locates the position of the houses of the zodiac in relation to the signs of the zodiac. The Ascendant is always the cusp, or first degree, of the 1st house.

Since the Ascendant stands on the border between light and shadow, it acts as the mediator between the day hemisphere of consciousness, objectivity, and direct influences, and the opposite night hemisphere of the unconscious, subjectivity, and indirect influences. It is the key to the personality, the total integrated self-awareness of the individual, including the state of physical health.

The nature of the Ascendant is largely influenced by the zodiac sign it occupies; therefore, the sign of the Ascendant will reveal the way the individual upon whom the reading is centered has accommodated his or her life to the environment. It describes both the way the world sees the individual, and the way the individual perceives him- or herself in relation to the world.

All the planets in the chart must be considered together with the Ascendant, which acts to focus their various influences into a single integrated wholeness.

Key: Personality and health

Descendant

The point where the ecliptic intersects the western horizon is the Descendant. The Sun occupies the Descendant at the moment of sunset, but it is better to think of the Descendant as the degree on the ecliptic that is sinking below the western horizon at any given time. The Descendant degree is always exactly opposite the Ascendant.

As the Ascendant represents the dawning of consciousness and the formation of personality, the Descendant is the setting of consciousness, the doorway into the world of dreams, suppressed urges and the unconscious, the dissolution of self-awareness.

The nature of the Descendant is largely determined by the sign it occupies. Planets in aspect with the Descendant will affect close interpersonal relationships.

The Descendant is generally considered to be less important than the Ascendant, and to be a balancing and complementary influence on the Ascendant.

Key: Close relationships, dreams

Midheaven

The intersection of the upper arc of the meridian with the ecliptic, the highest point on the ecliptic, is called *Medium Coeli*, or Midheaven. It corresponds with the position of the Sun at noon, but should not be thought of as bound to the orb of the Sun. In an ideal sense, it is at a right angle with the Ascendant, but in practice its location is usually more or less than 90 degrees from the Ascendant, depending upon the time of the year and time of day for which the chart is erected.

This variation occurs because, in the Northern Hemisphere, the signs from Cancer to Sagittarius take a longer period of time to ascend above the eastern horizon than the signs from Capricorn to Gemini. When a sign of long ascension is rising, the Midheaven is pushed into the 9th, or even the 8th, house. When a sign of short ascension is rising, the Midheaven will occupy the 10th or 11th house. When charts are cast for places nearer the equator, the variation of Midheaven from its ideal angle becomes smaller. In runic astrology we have no need to take this variation into account, and simply use the ideal location of Midheaven.

Planets located in the sign occupied by the Midheaven are the strongest, most direct, and explicit in their influence. The Midheaven is equivalent to the ego, or will, of the individual; it corresponds with the center and governor of consciousness. Planets in aspect with the Midheaven affect outward self-expression, social standing, and the career; and may involve an authority figure, possibly the father.

Key: Ego, will, authority

Lower Midheaven

Imum Coeli, or Lower Midheaven, is marked by the intersection of the lower arc of the meridian with the ecliptic, and in an astrological sense is the lowest point on the path of the Sun around the Earth. Lower Midheaven is exactly opposite Midheaven on the chart. It corresponds to the position of the Sun at midnight, deep on the far side of the Earth, but the Sun does not need to be in this place for the point of Midheaven to exist and to exert its influence.

Lower Midheaven is the center, or focus, of the unconscious, a kind of nadir-ego. Planets within the sign occupied by Lower Midheaven are weakest in their direct effect and act in a dark and subliminal manner. Planets in aspect with Lower Midheaven affect the home and family, all private and inward self-expression, and may involve the mother.

The effect of Lower Midheaven is generally considered to be less important than that of Midheaven, which it balances and complements.

Key: Unconscious, dark side

Nodes of the Moon

The North Node (ascending) of the Moon (☊) is called *caput draconus*, meaning the head of the dragon, and the South Node (descending) (☋) is called *cauda draconus*, meaning the tail of the dragon. These nodes are not heavenly bodies but points in space that move around the band of the zodiac once approximately every eighteen years, always directly opposite each other. The nodes are the places where the apparent circle, as viewed from Earth, that is traced by the orbit of the Moon intersects the apparent circle traced by the Sun.

For half of its monthly cycle, the Moon is below, or south, of the Sun's plane, called the ecliptic. For the other half of the time, it is above, or north, of the ecliptic. The exact spot the path of the Moon crosses the ecliptic going from south to north is called the ascending node (because the Moon is rising above the ecliptic), and the spot the path of the Moon crosses the ecliptic going from north to south is called the descending node (because the Moon is falling below the ecliptic).

It is important to understand that the nodes are not the places where the Moon itself intersects the ecliptic, but the places where the apparent orbit of the Moon crosses the apparent orbit of the Sun. The Moon does alternately occupy each node for a brief time in its course at roughly thirteen-day intervals, but the nodes continue to exist even when the Moon is not in them.

The role of the Moon is severely underestimated in modern Western astrology. This is curious since the Moon is the only heavenly body apart from the Sun that has an influence on life on Earth that is manifest and measurable. Astrologers in Europe and North America tend to minimize the importance of the lunar phases, lunar eclipses, and the lunar nodes. This is not true of astrologers in India, where the Moon receives its due measure of importance.

It is not generally realized that the nodes of the Moon are composed of the simple qualities of the Sun and Moon, and therefore are an essential balancing influence in the astrological chart to the planet pairs Venus-Mars (Sun-Earth qualities), and Jupiter-Saturn (Moon-Earth qualities).

The makeup of the nodes is suggested by their glyphs, which consist of two circles connected by a crescent. In the ascending node, or North Node, the crescent is elevated above the circles, indicating that the lunar quality dominates the solar; in the descending node, or South Node, the circles are elevated above the crescent, indicating that the solar quality dominates the lunar. Each small circle in the glyphs of the lunar nodes marks where the path of the Moon intersects the path of the Sun. The crescents in the glyphs describe the arc traced by the Moon, either above or below the plane of the ecliptic.

The nodes always act in concert with each other. They are permanently locked in the aspect of opposition, separated by 180 degrees, indicating the dynamic interplay between them. An aspect formed with one node will be balanced by a complementary aspect formed with the other node. As the ascending node gives, the descending node takes at the same time and to an equal degree.

North Node (Ascending)

Traditionally, the head of the dragon signifies good fortune. An understanding of why this is so can be gained by examining the makeup of its glyph. The North Node is soul (lunar crescent) dominant over spirit (solar circle). It is the mental aspect of self harnessing the universal spiritual force, which is made to manifest in the events of life through flashes of higher awareness, insights, fortunate or happy choices and decisions, lucky picks and guesses, being in the right place at the right time, landing on one's feet, and so on.

The very symbolism of a head suggests the forward-looking, intellectual, willful, purposeful role of this node. A head advances and projects. The plane of the ecliptic may be regarded as the surface of the sea that divides the conscious airy heights from the unconscious watery depths. When the Moon rises above this plane at the ascending node, it indicates a positive, giving, conscious energy acting in an individual and human manner—creativity expressed in a personal way. The vitality of spirit is made to serve or express itself through the individual will for purposes that are important to human consciousness. Therefore, the ascending node signifies good fortune from a human viewpoint.

Key: Good fortune, giving, elevation, revealing

South Node (Descending)

The South Node has traditionally been held to signify evil fortune. The explanation lies in the structure of its glyph. The South Node is spirit (solar circle) over soul (lunar crescent). It is the universal mind controlling the individual awareness, which results in a life that is tossed about by higher forces like a bottle on the waves of the ocean. Anyone falling under this influence will be a tool of Fate, a pawn in a larger game with little control over matters that are of a purely human dimension. Control is snatched out of the hands of the individual who must then endure events, come what will.

The very symbolism of the South Node, or tail, suggests the passive, receptive, feeling nature of this node, that it is something drawn along or led. A tail also covers or conceals. When the Moon falls below the plane of the ecliptic it indicates a negative, demanding, pitiless, unconscious energy acting in a universal, spiritual manner. Creativity and personal expression are suppressed in favor of universal consciousness, generally perceived as evil by humanity because it makes the individual will subordinate to divine will, or destiny, which cannot be comprehended by limited human awareness. Little wonder this influence is seen to be unlucky.

Key: Bad fortune, taking, repression, concealing

10

The Aspects

Astrologers relate the actions of the planets to each other through the use of aspects, which are angular distances between points on the ecliptic as measured from Earth; or, in the astrological chart, angular distances between points on the circumference of the zodiac circle measured from its center. Only specific angles are considered to be significant—the other angles are ignored. Aspects affect in different ways the interaction of the planets located on the aspect angles, as well as the signs and houses they occupy, in some cases creating harmony between them, in other cases producing conflict. These simple aspects are illustrated in Figure 10-1.

An aspect can be measured on both sides from any degree occupied by a planet or significant astrological point such as a lunar node. Remember that the angles between planets are actually measured from the center of the chart. The conventional methods for showing the aspects on the chart do not really make this clear. All the degrees that can potentially be in simple aspect with the 15th degree of Capricorn are shown in Figure 10-2.

Because runic astrology presumes an ideal movement of the planets, the aspect known as parallel, which exists when two or more planets have the same angular distance in declination north or south of the celestial equator, is not used.

Also, since the oracle will only place planets with an accuracy of 5 degrees, planets are considered to be in aspect when the quines they occupy are in aspect. The whole question of orbs—maximum angular distances planets can deviate from the perfect aspect angles yet still be considered to be in aspect—does not apply to runic astrology. The exception to this

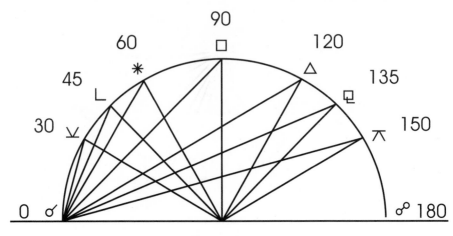

Figure 10-1

rule is conjunction. In runic astrology, planets are considered to be in conjunction if they occupy the same quine, or adjacent quines.

Major aspects are those that exert a powerful or moderately powerful influence; minor aspects are those whose influence is weak. Easy aspects have a generally harmonious and helpful influence; difficult aspects produce discordance and have a hindering effect. However, no aspect is in itself either good or bad. Whether its influence is beneficial or difficult depends on the circumstances that surround it.

Easy aspects result from divisions of the circle of the zodiac by three and its multiples, resulting in the trine family of aspects. Difficult aspects arise from divisions of the zodiac by four and its multiples, resulting in the square family of aspects. This distinction is based upon occult numerology. One is harmonious, two is discordant, three is spiritual, four is material—to understand this is to grasp the root of the astrological aspects.

There are other recognized aspects based upon dividing the zodiac into five and nine, but these are little used and fall outside the purview of this basic treatment, which is intended only to serve as a practical guide for the runic astrology oracle. Anyone who wishes to employ these less common aspects in interpreting the chart can easily do so by entering them on the small blank chart along with all the other aspects.

It will be noticed by those with a knowledge of astrology that certain aspects can occur in the runic astrology oracle that will never be duplicated by the actual planets in the heavens due to the limitations of their orbits about the Sun. For example, in a conventional astrology chart, Venus will never be found in square, trine, or opposition to Mercury in

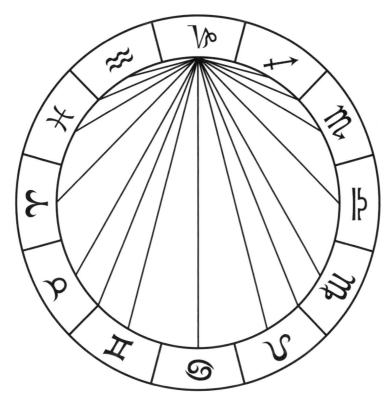

Figure 10-2

the heavens because both these inner planets orbit near the Sun and always stay within 76 degrees of each other. By the same token, the Sun cannot be in trine to Venus (the two are never more than 48 degrees apart) or in semisquare to Mercury (they are never more than 28 degrees apart).

In runic astrology, these strictly theoretical aspects can and do happen. This may be looked upon as either a defect or a virtue of the oracle, depending on how closely you believe the system of interacting astrological symbols is tied to the actual planetary and stellar bodies they represent. I happen to believe that the elegant and beautiful art of astrology has almost nothing to do with the science of astronomy. True, the physical planets and stars acted as the source of inspiration for astrology at its primal beginning, but over the centuries astrology struck out on its own independent course. Astrology is no more dependant upon the stars than the Chinese system of divination known as the I Ching is dependant upon yarrow sticks.

With every planet potentially able to enter into every aspect with all other planets, a whole new world of interpretation is unlocked that was forever sealed to regular astrology. Adding these variables increases the subtlety of the reading and makes it possible to apply it more directly to specific circumstances, sharpening its focus. It is as though a gate has been opened into a previously forbidden zone of astrological analysis.

Conjunction

Angle: 0°

Glyph: ☌

Type: Major

Kind: Easy

Planets are in conjunction when they occupy the same or adjacent quines. This aspect indicates a point of focus that emphasizes the qualities of the joined planets and causes them to act in unison. Planets in conjunction are bound together, their powers fused into a single combined force. It is usually difficult to separate their effects. When they occupy the same quine, their action should generally be regarded as more powerful than when they are in adjacent quines. If a perfect conjunction exists, the glyphs of the conjoined planets should be written one above the other on the small blank chart in the open space beneath their sign, signifying that they lie in the same quine.

Opposition

Angle: 180°

Glyph: ☍

Type: Major

Kind: Difficult

An opposition exists when planets are located in quines separated by 180 degrees. It is an important and powerful aspect indicating tension, usually of an unfavorable kind because it opposes the action of one planet with another, creating stress. This aspect can reveal inner conflict that may lie hidden beneath the surface. If the planets complement rather than oppose each other, the effect can be positive.

The Secret Doctrine
Vol 1 & 2   *28.00*

Masks of Odin 19.00

www. Natvanbooks. com

3.00

harmony and ease of action, signifying good fortune where
...cupy are concerned; and balanced relationships, situations
...pful but tend to be static and lack motivation. This aspect
... line of least resistance; perhaps a personal habit.

Sextile

Angle: 60°

Glyph: ✶

Type: Minor

Kind: Easy

The sextile is an aspect of moderate potency that is one of the trine family of aspects.
It is generally positive but its harmony is less strong and less perfect than the trine from
which it is derived. Because this aspect links signs of the same polarity, positive to positive
and negative to negative, it frequently involves relationships between the same sex of an
intellectual or esthetic nature, generally of an impersonal type.

Semisextile

Angle: 30°

Glyph: ⊻

Type: Minor

Kind: Easy

There is doubt as to the effect of this minor, weak aspect. Since it is a multiple of the
trine (3 X 4 = 12) it might be expected to be favorable; however, it can also be regarded as a
multiple of the square (4 X 3 = 12) which would render it unfavorable. It involves adjacent
signs, which have no natural accord in polarity, quality, or element, further compounding
the difficulty. Margaret Hone wrote that older books describe this aspect as "weakly good,"[1]
and this seems to me as good a description as any.

Quincunx

Angle: 150°
Glyph: ⚻
Type: Minor
Kind: Easy

The quincunx is a minor aspect made up of five semisextiles, and it is referred to as a harmonic of the trine and sextile because it is based upon multiples of a threefold division of the zodiac. As one of the trine family, it indicates slightly harmonious relationships. However, the signs in quincunx, like those in semisextile, share no correspondences of polarity, quality, or element; therefore, this aspect might equally be regarded as one of minor strain. Perhaps this lack of correspondence is responsible for the other name of this aspect, which is also called the inconjunct.

Square

Angle: 90°
Glyph: □
Type: Major
Kind: Difficult

The square is a potent aspect that has an obstructive and disruptive effect. At the same time, it is dynamic and releases much motivational energy that can be employed for creative purposes. Square aspects provoke action as a response to contradiction and liberate personal power from the depths of the soul. Too many square aspects, however, indicate great difficulties that may be insurmountable, or at least will require extraordinary effort to overcome and will leave lasting scars.

Semisquare

Angle: 45°
Glyph: ∟
Type: Minor
Kind: Difficult

A minor aspect that results when the square is divided in half. It indicates difficulties and tensions of a not too serious nature; obstructions that can be overcome with honest effort.

Sesquiquadrate

Angle: 135°

Glyph: ⟁

Type: Minor

Kind: Difficult

As its glyph implies, sesquiquadrate is the square plus the semisquare measure, which produces minor strain that can be overcome with effort and a positive attitude. The semisquare and the sesquiquadrate (also called the sesquisquare) are related, since both are produced by a division of the zodiac into eight parts.

In addition to these simple aspects, there are three compound aspects, formed by adding major aspects together, which are of the highest importance in reading the chart. They are called the grand trine, grand cross, and T-square. Any time one of these compound aspects is found in the chart, it dominates the interpretation. Figure 10-3 illustrates their structure.

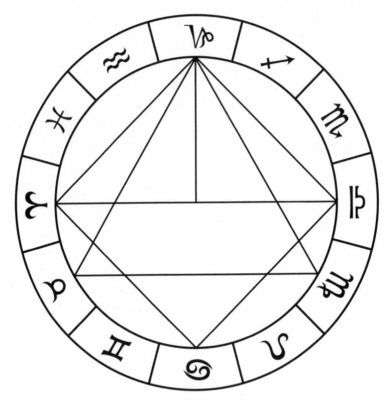

Figure 10-3

Grand Trine

The grand trine is formed by three trine aspects involving three or more planets or significant points, which create the pattern of a large equilateral triangle within the circle of the zodiac. This intensifies the harmonizing influence that is natural to trine aspects and generates an easy personal climate, free of opposition or the need to struggle. If more than three planets are involved in the aspect, which can occur if there is a conjunction at one or more of the points of the triangle, the element of the three signs touched by the triangle may be over-accentuated, creating an imbalance. An excess of good fortune brought on by the grand trine may prove too much for persons of weak character, causing them to become lazy and parasitical.

Grand Cross

The grand cross is formed by four square aspects involving four or more planets or significant points that create the pattern of a large square, or cross, within the circle of the zodiac. This generates great disruption and conflict, resulting in a life or circumstance that is anything but dull. This tribulation can either break or temper the spirit of the one who must endure it. A cross on the fixed signs suggests that the person involved will try to accommodate the difficulties and make the best of a bad lot; a cross on cardinal signs means the person will attempt to overcome the problems; a cross on mutable signs indicates that the person will seek to get around the obstacles without actually dealing with them, which may result in a breakdown or other disorder born of frustration.

T-Square

The T-square exists when two planets in opposition are each in square aspect to a third planet. The tension of opposition is complicated and aggravated by the third planet, which adds its problems to the situation. Often insight may be gained concerning the solution to the difficulties by considering the missing leg of the incomplete grand cross represented in the T-square pattern. The point where the fourth leg of the cross would touch may be of great importance by virtue of its omission.

Planets in the Signs and Houses

In the beginning it is convenient to have a list of significant descriptive words and phrases that can be applied to the planets, Ascendant, Midheaven, and North Node of the Moon, according to their location in the signs and houses. These provide a starting point in interpreting the chart, but should not be considered sufficient to obtain a complete analysis. The diviner must refer back to the detailed descriptions of the signs, houses, and planets in order to flesh out these skeletal meanings.

It will be noticed that the same adjectives often occur under different zodiac signs. None of these words has a definitive and exclusive association. Each has many shades of meaning and can be interpreted in various ways depending upon its context. For the fullest and clearest understanding of either the positive or negative nature of a planet in a particular sign, take all four descriptive words and consider them together for their collective unique sense.

Only the positive poles of the three pairs of opposing significant points (which are the Ascendant/Descendant, the Midheaven/Lower Midheaven, and North Node/South Node pairs) are listed below. The meaning of the corresponding negative poles can be gained by considering the positive pole definition for a particular sign or house, and modifying it according to the key meaning of the negative pole.

For example, the Ascendant in Scorpio signifies, among other things, the outward expression of passion, because the key to the Ascendant is the personality, or persona—the personal mask the individual presents to the world. But the key of the Descendant is intimate relationships and dreams. Therefore, the Descendant in Scorpio may signify, among other things, private or intimate passions and strong fantasies. The key to the Midheaven is the ego, or true self. Midheaven in Scorpio signifies that passion is a defining feature of the essential nature. The key to Lower Midheaven is the unconscious, indicating that the Lower Midheaven in Scorpio may mean suppressed or destructive passions.

The four positive words under each sign apply to the planets when they are well aspected in that sign. The four alternative negative words apply to the planets when they are poorly aspected. The meanings for the houses are general. They should be given a favorable interpretation when the planet in the house is in easy aspect, and an unfavorable emphasis when the planet is in difficult aspect.

Ascendant

Key: Personality

By Sign

Aries: Assertive, ambitious, forceful, independent
Rash, aggressive, quarrelsome, violent

Taurus: Attractive, sensual, practical, harmonious
Obstinate, taciturn, indulgent, dogmatic

Gemini: Quick, versatile, vivacious, adaptable
Inconstant, ruthless, superficial, nervous

Cancer: Protective, impressionable, gentle, affectionate
Introverted, humble, dependent, moody

Leo: Confident, impressive, noble, motivated
Arrogant, pretentious, pushy, vainglorious

Virgo: Discreet, precise, reserved, painstaking
Pedantic, prejudiced, anxious, punctilious

Libra: Charming, sociable, relaxed, agreeable
Indolent, vain, gushing, insincere

Scorpio: Aggressive, hot-blooded, impulsive, willful
Violent, deep, lustful, secretive

Sagittarius: Expansive, adventurous, independent, lively
Careless, messy, garrulous, undependable

Capricorn: Tenacious, pragmatic, ambitious, reserved
   Unhappy, lonely, bitter, anxious

Aquarius: Outgoing, expressive, friendly, reasonable
   Shallow, cool, eccentric, detached

Pisces: Quiet, receptive, passive, sympathetic
   Lazy, vague, weak, depressed

By House

1st: Need to assert identity; active personal environment

2nd: Concern about appearance; need to create harmonious environment through beautiful possessions

3rd: Personality expresses itself verbally or intellectually; need to relate to those in the immediate circle

4th: Fulfillment in home life; personal identity expressed within the family; concern about providing necessities of life for others

5th: Leadership in games, sports, speculative ventures; pleasure in testing limits of self; artistry

6th: Health and hygiene are personally important; fulfillment in work of a practical type

7th: Happiness in a harmonious, pleasant marriage; partnership that requires little personal effort

8th: Aggressive, potentially violent personal environment; fascination with mystical matters; preoccupation with sexuality and proving oneself

9th: Intense personal need to expand horizons through knowledge; travel; restless search for meaning

10th: Attempts to prove oneself in the professional world; establishing a reputation; impressing those in authority

11th: Identifying oneself with a class or group; group objectives take precedence over individual goals; loss of self in collective movement

12th: Personal need for privacy; solitary examination of emotions and thoughts; weak personal identity

Midheaven

Key: Ego

By Sign

Aries: Confident, aware, established, decided
  Conceited, hasty, domineering, selfish

Taurus: Persistent, tenacious, conservative, patient
  Plodding, stubborn, unsatisfied, willful

Gemini: Talented, versatile, eclectic, multiple
  Facile, unstable, dilatory, indecisive

Cancer: Modest, thrifty, simple, responsible
  Avaricious, clinging, moody, emotional

Leo: Optimistic, confident, ambitious, proud
  Domineering, rigid, egotistical, selfish

Virgo: Organized, practical, moral, reserved
  Hypersensitive, petty, vain, calculated

Libra: Diplomatic, harmonious, cooperative, fortunate
  Manipulating, exploitative, artificial, vainglorious

Scorpio: Purposeful, independent, acquisitive, energetic
  Domineering, destructive, compulsive, ruthless

Sagittarius: Aspiring, idealistic, optimistic, futuristic
  Utopian, impractical, undependable, changeable

Capricorn: Ambitious, driven, tenacious, conscientious
  Prosaic, selfish, self-centered, lonely

Aquarius: Innovative, aspiring, modern, liberated
  Vague, unrealistic, undisciplined, unfocused

Pisces: Gentle, patient, tolerant, meditative
  Impressionable, passive, unambitious, procrastinating

By House

1st: Confident awareness of essential identity; aggressive pursuit of goals

2nd: Steady but persistent building of a personal life with clear awareness of the necessary
  steps; pursuit of a secure material expression of identity

3rd: Aims in life are many and shifting; division of attention; becoming tangled in the goals of others

4th: Sense of self strongly tied to the family; home provides outlet for true identity

5th: Social prominence; self-confidence in higher social circles; a sense of having arrived

6th: Intellectual profession; identifying self with caring for basic needs of others; putting self into work

7th: Identity expresses itself through another; manipulation behind the scenes; agent-client relationship

8th: A self consumed by passions; mediumship; identification with one who is dead

9th: Identification with distant places or far-off times; study of ancient languages; adopting citizenship of nation culturally distant; futurist; archaeology

10th: Self-confidence in profession; willingness to assume command; leadership role; self-assurance in strength of professional track record

11th: Devotion heart and soul to intellectual ideals and humanitarian goals; leading a reforming society or consciousness group

12th: Lack of understanding where true identity lies; confusion about life goals and directions; contemplative religious life or withdrawal from society

Sun

Key: Self-expression

By Sign

Aries: Bold, energetic, assertive, single-minded
  Harsh, crude, selfish, combative

Taurus: Conservative, resourceful, hospitable, productive
  Stubborn, possessive, material, grasping

Gemini: Versatile, communicative, lively, adaptive
  Restless, unfocused, excitable, superficial

Cancer: Protective, emotional, domestic, conserving
  Irrational, moody, retiring, withholding

Leo: Powerful, cheerful, proud, magnanimous
  Despotic, conceited, snobbish, wasteful

Virgo: Practical, modest, discriminating, careful
  Interfering, fussy, distant, critical

Libra: Companionable, pleasant, easygoing, artistic
  Indecisive, discontented, uncertain, indolent

Scorpio: Passionate, secretive, penetrating, enduring
  Resentful, vengeful, brooding, obstinate

Sagittarius: Idealistic, optimistic, restless, enthusiastic
  Unsettled, careless, extravagant, inconsiderate

Capricorn: Calculating, cautious, responsible, reserved
  Selfish, inhibited, unresponsive, worrying

Aquarius: Unconventional, independent, original, detached
  Perverse, rebellious, erratic, inconstant

Pisces: Impressionable, intuitive, sympathetic, sacrificing
  Deceitful, timid, impractical, secretive

By House

1st: Important personal affairs; light cast on life situation; concentration on self; personal insights

2nd: Earning money; desire for wealth; preoccupation with valuables; strong personal feelings

3rd: Mental activity and communication vitalized; travel for personal reasons; success through modifications; connection with neighbors and siblings

4th: Happiness at home; self-fulfillment in family setting; meeting essential needs

5th: Success and personal happiness with love affairs; siring of children; games; sports; artistic creations

6th: Excellent health; physical strength; aptitude for work; good employee relations

7th: Successful marriage; profitable partnership

8th: Success with the opposite sex; strong desires expressed; skill and enjoyment in love-making; normal death

9th: Residence overseas; profit from study; intellectual dedication; love of books or travel

10th: Social prominence; success with career; worldly honors; personal authority

11th: Focus on group goals; pleasure in clubs and social organizations; commitment to politics

12th: Hidden personal development; psychic ability; strong intuitions; devotion of the self to others

Moon

Key: Rhythmic response

By Sign

Aries: Restless, insistent, excitable, reactive
   Thoughtless, abrupt, irritable, impatient

Taurus: Tactile, sympathetic, subdued, tranquil
   Acquisitive, over-sensitive, melancholy, mothering

Gemini: Adaptive, manifold, versatile, mobile
   Inconsistent, contradictory, two-faced, unsettled

Cancer: Domestic, devoted, maternal, receptive
   Clannish, dependent, unstable, impressionable

Leo: Confident, generous, magnanimous, luxurious
   Hedonistic, ostentations, aggrandizing, self-satisfied

Virgo: Meticulous, reserved, correct, modest
   Prudish, anxious, fastidious, nervous

Libra: Romantic, courteous, affectionate, compromising
   Dependent, fickle, flighty, capricious

Scorpio: Emotional, deep, possessive, intense
   Jealous, obstinate, vicious, one-sided

Sagittarius: Sincere, sociable, alert, frank
   Inconsistent, careless, restless, changeable

Capricorn: Steadfast, reserved, sensible, patient
   Reticent, apprehensive, pessimistic, inhibited

Aquarius: Innovative, humane, civilized, detached
   Inane, erratic, superficial, aloof

Pisces: Dreamy, vulnerable, psychic, yielding
   Dependent, moody, self-doubting, shy

By House

1st: Vicissitudes in personal affairs; changeable nature; desire for travel; strong personality

2nd: Shift in feelings; alteration of financial situation; material dealings with women; acquisitions

3rd: A shift in early education; lack of commitment; upheaval in relations with brother or sister; hurried purposeless activity; much ado about nothing

4th: Affairs of the home; concerns over the family situation; change in residence; interest in hereditary or bloodline

5th: Relations with women; health of children; interest in literature or art; gambling winnings and losses

6th: Interest in state of health; hypochondria; seasonal disorders; allergies; concern for public hygiene; seeking or finding employment for others

7th: Changeable intimate relationship; desire for a maternal spouse; friendships with women; pursuit of pleasure

8th: Interest in sexual matters; psychic research; the afterlife; mediumship; legacies; service as a trustee or executor

9th: Occult studies; interest in medicine and healing; philosophy; travel by or over water; study of the sea

10th: A public life; preoccupation with career; family responsibilities

11th: Indiscriminate joining of groups; political or idealistic infatuation; lack of commitment limits success in organized activity

12th: Retirement; work carried out in seclusion; spirit communication; works of the imagination; drug or alcohol problem

Mercury

Key: Communication

By Sign

Aries: Assertive, witty, eloquent, frank
　　Sarcastic, cutting, quarrelsome, tactless

Taurus: Deliberate, sensible, thorough, formal
　　Ponderous, dogmatic, stodgy, prejudiced

Gemini: Versatile, fluent, clever, inquisitive
Verbose, flippant, facile, gossipy

Cancer: Intuitive, impressionable, retentive, perceptive
Irrational, narrow-minded, reactionary, sentimental

Leo: Outspoken, determined, expansive, aspiring
Voluble, conceited, arrogant, bossy

Virgo: Discerning, analytical, assimilative, precise
Worrisome, fussy, hypercritical, skeptical

Libra: Charming, well-spoken, balanced, scholarly
Vapid, unoriginal, indecisive, weak-willed

Scorpio: Probing, focused, perceptive, intense
Acidic, sharp, insulting, sarcastic

Sagittarius: Sincere, free-spoken, open-minded, versatile
Garrulous, inconstant, diffuse, irreverent

Capricorn: Ambitious, logical, serious, deliberate
Procrastinating, exacting, censorious, suspicious

Aquarius: Inventive, progressive, inquisitive, involved
Utopian, eccentric, unrealistic, contrary

Pisces: Impressionable, discursive, imaginative, creative
Gullible, irrational, changeable, indecisive

By House

1st: Rational approach to personal affairs; attention to mental studies and diversions; analytical self-examination

2nd: Money management; accounting; investment; clerical work

3rd: Correspondence; writing; reading; nervous troubles caused by worry; communication with brother or sister

4th: Study at home; domestic business activities; interest in collecting; cataloging of possessions

5th: Creative writing, reading, or narrating of poetry and literature; diaries and journals; autobiography; lovers; pleasures; intellectual concerns with children

6th: Worry about daily work and health; employment in secretarial, commercial, and educational fields

7th: Communication with partner in business or marriage concerning rapport; reciprocity; balance

8th: Envy for the possessions or wealth of others; deep thoughts and strong feelings; jealousy; desire to possess; attraction to forbidden knowledge

9th: Restless urge to travel; interest in foreign languages and cultures; intellectual quests

10th: Practical interest in business or politics; fame for profit rather than glamour

11th: Intellectual friendships; pursuit of scientific or social goals; correspondence with groups; meetings of like minds; letters or articles to club newsletters

12th: Solitary occult study; secret communications; private mental odyssey; excursions on the water; prayer

Venus

Key: Cooperation

By Sign

Aries: Demonstrative, generous, ardent, persuasive
Selfish, self-centered, headstrong, erotic

Taurus: Faithful, affectionate, artistic, conservative
Indolent, possessive, materialistic, greedy

Gemini: Charming, courteous, adaptable, pleasant
Ingratiating, superficial, silly, flirtatious

Cancer: Tender, devoted, romantic, indulgent
Dependent, demanding, vain, dreamy

Leo: Generous, merry, vivacious, artistic
Hedonistic, extravagant, proud, luxurious

Virgo: Modest, restrained, polite, decorous
Repressed, fastidious, dissatisfied, discriminative

Libra: Attractive, companionable, charming, lively
Frivolous, discontented, trifling, mawkish

Scorpio: Magnetic, erotic, intense, secretive
  Licentious, depraved, jealous, obsessive

Sagittarius: Bright, independent, attractive, demonstrative
  Unstable, scattered, inconsiderate, lewd

Capricorn: Constant, formal, sincere, stable
  Joyless, stern, distrustful, unfeeling

Aquarius: Progressive, refined, friendly, detached
  Libertine, cool, unconventional, superficial

Pisces: Submissive, indulgent, tender, giving
  Exploitable, sentimental, soft, weak

By House

1st: Attraction to pleasures; social amusements; beautiful people; glamour

2nd: Esthetic employment through the marketing or sale of art; clothing; flowers; interior designs; jewelry; cosmetics

3rd: Social visits; studies for pleasure or entertainment; shallow but pleasant relations with siblings; parties

4th: Home decorating; remodeling; delight in ornaments and furnishings; harmonious emotional relations with family

5th: Happiness and success in love affairs; beautiful children; enjoyment of theatrics and public performance; success in games

6th: Talent for motivating others; joy in work; harmonious relations; smooth progress; good health; need for a clean and attractive environment

7th: Harmonious and loving marriage; ability to get along with others; smooth business partnership

8th: Fulfilling sex life; profit from a partnership; an easy death; pleasure in spiritual pursuits; inheritance

9th: Success or profit from overseas or foreigners; marriage to a foreigner; living abroad; vacationing and travel for pleasure

10th: Success in career; happy public life; skill at diplomacy; good relations with parents

11th: Skill at organizing or running charities, clubs or groups; pleasant social circle; like-minded friends

12th: Enjoyment of solitude; secluded retreat; secret love affair; pleasure in mystery; liking for the occult; a clear and untroubled unconscious mind

Mars
Key: Assertion of self

By Sign
Aries: Assertive, aggressive, energetic, courageous
  Domineering, violent, reckless, brutal
Taurus: Tenacious, industrious, acquisitive, determined
  Obstinate, surly, vindictive, sensual
Gemini: Talkative, energetic, agile, adept
  Quarrelsome, irreverent, high-strung, mischievous
Cancer: Ambitious, impulsive, instinctual, tenacious
  Irritable, temperamental, reactive, inconstant
Leo: Initiating, audacious, formative, dramatic
  Ruthless, domineering, egotistic, melodramatic
Virgo: Ingenious, painstaking, energetic, orderly
  Exploitative, interfering, compulsive, nitpicking
Libra: Persuasive, associative, ardent, affectionate
  Disputatious, vulgar, offensive, blunt
Scorpio: Irresistible, powerful, ambitious, sexual
  Sadistic, dissipated, destructive, vengeful
Sagittarius: Competitive, explorative, bold, independent
  Impetuous, extravagant, uncontrolled, boisterous
Capricorn: Industrious, authoritative, ambitious, determined
  Authoritarian, malicious, defiant, restless
Aquarius: Spirited, independent, enthusiastic, progressive
  Rebellious, impatient, contradictory, perverse
Pisces: Generous, emotional, sacrificing, zealous
  Depraved, poisonous, unstable, procrastinating

By House

1st: Initiation of personal enterprise; forceful action; personal combat or dispute

2nd: New business venture; planting of seeds; executive position

3rd: Work in education; literature; restless activity; brother or sister demands attention

4th: Intense activity within the home; possible domestic strife or hardship

5th: Rough play and sports; aggressive pursuit of sexual partners; active pleasures

6th: Hard work; demanding employment; severe taskmaster; possibly a fever or stroke

7th: Competition within partnership or marriage; quarrels; rivalry

8th: Concern in financial affairs of another; preoccupation with sex life; psychic research; interest in surgery or psychotherapy

9th: Passion for unconventional recreations and games; search for meaning in life

10th: Climbing the corporate ladder; competition in career; promotion; advancement

11th: Novel interests; new friends; taking up of causes with little commitment; embracing new ideas and discarding old ones

12th: Altruistic actions; secret charity; repayment in kind; can be hidden malice

Jupiter

Key: Expansion

By Sign

Aries: Generous, noble, self-sufficient, capable
   Extravagant, overbearing, boastful, speculating

Taurus: Jovial, reliable, good-hearted, liberal
   Greedy, wasteful, exploitative, self-indulgent

Gemini: Obliging, carefree, versatile, talkative
   Hypocritical, conceited, opinionated, empty

Cancer: Sympathetic, kindly, protective, charitable
   Manipulative, over-attached, touchy, smothering

Leo: Lofty, noble, loyal, big-hearted
   Pretentious, vain, inflated, overbearing

Virgo: Ethical, honest, professional, discerning
   Amoral, cynical, rationalizing, sophistical

Libra: Just, merciful, philanthropic, companionable
   Dependent, capricious, conceited, indolent

Scorpio: Proud, subtle, shrewd, deep
   Pleasure-loving, self-indulgent, headstrong, forceful

Sagittarius: Generous, dignified, freedom-loving, tolerant
   Lawless, wasteful, exaggerating, chaotic

Capricorn: Careful, far-sighted, organized, responsible
   Austere, egocentric, self-righteous, narrow

Aquarius: Humane, sympathetic, liberal, obliging
   Intolerant, anarchistic, careless, unkind

Pisces: Benevolent, altruistic, generous, visionary
   Indolent, extravagant, fantasizing, unreliable

By House

1st: Opportunities for growth; personal good fortune

2nd: Financial success; pleasure in the good things of life

3rd: Successful communication; profit through writings; an active, capable intellect; advantageous relations with siblings

4th: Comfortable home life; good relations with parents; family will prosper

5th: Speculations and risk-taking will be fruitful under good aspect; children prosperous; enjoyment of sports

6th: Robust health; plentiful employment opportunities; cheerful employee relations

7th: Fortunate or rich marriage; lucrative and happy partnership

8th: Easy death; legacy; also prosperity through marriage; close relationship in business or social setting

9th: Success in profound studies; happy life abroad; profitable dealings with foreigners

10th: Success with ease in worldly affairs; professional prosperity; good opportunities for growth and advancement

11th: Many friends and acquaintances; enjoyment of the society of others; fulfillment of goals

12th: Profit from the sea; secret charity work; success in the performing arts, probably as one behind the scenes

Saturn

Key: Limitation

By Sign

Aries: Ambitious, diligent, self-reliant, enduring
 Impatient, irresponsible, defiant, unsympathetic

Taurus: Methodical, constructive, stable, cautious
 Miserly, inhibited, dour, materialistic

Gemini: Calculating, abstract, detached, scientific
 Awkward, slow, cold, negative

Cancer: Shrewd, cautious, self-centered, guarding
 Repressed, selfish, grasping, resentful

Leo: Assured, responsible, determined, authoritative
 Ungratified, frustrated, shy, unhappy

Virgo: Punctilious, methodical, precise, meticulous
 Dogmatic, nagging, exacting, hypercritical

Libra: Dutiful, conscientious, reliable, impartial
 Impractical, constrained, inhibited, insincere

Scorpio: Resourceful, purposeful, reserved, cautious
 Morose, twisted, selfish, brooding

Sagittarius: Dignified, sincere, studious, determined
 Censorious, joyless, insincere, uncertain

Capricorn: Disciplined, ambitious, restrained, patient
 Cold, depressed, selfish, pessimistic

Aquarius: Rational, controlled, deliberate, sincere
 Fanatical, deceitful, cunning, withdrawn

Pisces: Isolated, long-suffering, modest, serious
 Melancholic, self-pitying, fearful, unfulfilled

By House

1st: Insecurity; feelings of inadequacy; heavy responsibilities and burdens; depression

2nd: Financial cares; sensible ordering of property; concern about possessions; need to set limits on buying

3rd: Gap in education; limits on correspondence or communication; acceptance of responsibility for brother or sister

4th: Caring for health of parents; harshness or austerity at home; maintaining the home residence; housing costs

5th: Delay in pleasure; frustration; love problems; responsibility for children; attraction to an older person

6th: Health problems; difficulties with employees or work environment; problems in meeting contracts or quotas

7th: Marriage difficulties; divorce; breakup or troubles with business partnership; difficulty in forming close relationships

8th: Losses caused by others; need to assume responsibility; serious sexual liaison; sexual dysfunction; thoughts of death

9th: Vacation difficulties; travel delays; frustration in travel arrangements; duty trips; questioning of beliefs

10th: Need for serious application to career; slow progress; delays in advancement; family burdens intensify efforts

11th: Affinity for older friends; friendships transitory or shallow; focus on concrete life objectives that may be elusive

12th: Depression; suffering borne in secret; miserable life; self-pity; suicidal tendencies

North Node

Key: Elevation

By Sign

Aries: Enthusiastic, ardent, expressive, sociable
   Domineering, extroverted, lascivious, pompous

Taurus: Devoted, loyal, reliable, skillful
   Exploitative, self-seeking, sensual, acquisitive

Gemini: Intelligent, articulate, perceptive, persuasive
Opportunistic, parasitical, transitory, variable

Cancer: Attached, obliging, giving, domestic
Dependent, unadventurous, guarded, defensive

Leo: Generous, fortunate, cheerful, popular
Wasteful, risk-taking, conceited, boisterous

Virgo: Practical, methodical, productive, conservative
Critical, withdrawn, meddling, fastidious

Libra: Communal, agreeable, attractive, charming
Dependent, demanding, indolent, flattering

Scorpio: Potent, enduring, forceful, willful
Destructive, violent, brutal, perverse

Sagittarius: Academic, idealistic, advanced, optimistic
Utopian, unrealistic, undependable, vague

Capricorn: Clear, determined, authoritative, resourceful
Arrogant, snobbish, exploitative, deceiving

Aquarius: Sociable, engaging, abstract, intellectual
Dependent, aloof, scattered, indifferent

Pisces: Empathetic, dreamy, visionary, charitable
Secretive, moody, depressed, indolent

By House

1st: Forms of self-expression; the need to command and organize

2nd: Long-term alliances; money or gifts from others; successful unions

3rd: Benefiting from relatives, neighbors; pleasant superficial relationships; lively exchange of ideas

4th: Giving family situation; support from parents; soul mates; interesting ancestry

5th: Gambling; speculations with others; many children; entertainments; festivals

6th: Animal or laboratory research; work with drugs, cosmetics; science; education; teaching; useful services

7th: Love affair leading to marriage; long-term partnership; teamwork; public service

8th: Political or religious associations; secret relations; subversive groups or individual; sexual obsession

9th: Educational or humanitarian aims; utopian goals; physical or spiritual voyages

10th: Business organizations; boards; committees; position of authority; situations of responsibility

11th: Many friends and acquaintances; offering to help without true commitment; clubs; groups; love of social contacts

12th: Occult group; retirement or contemplative community; secret societies; hidden enemies; confining or restraining conditions

Aspects of the Planets

The following description of the aspects that occur between the planets, Ascendant, Midheaven, and ascending node of the Moon in the runic astrology chart is intended only for quick reference to refresh the memory. It should not be regarded as all-inclusive. There is much more that might be said about various individual aspects, and these can only be thoroughly understood through repeated consideration of them in the wide variety of circumstances that arise in actual charts.

Some of the aspects described here are ideal, or symbolic. They will never occur in the actual heavens. The inclusion of these ideal aspects fills many interpretive gaps that exist in conventional astrology. For example, there has always been a place in the symbolic framework of the horoscope for a Sun in opposition to Mercury aspect, and the meaning of this aspect is not invalidated simply because it is physically impossible due to the close orbit of Mercury about the Sun. In runic astrology, this potential expansion of interpretation is fulfilled.

The descriptions under conjunction also apply to easy and difficult aspects, but in the easy aspects (trine, sextile, semisextile, quincunx) the working of these factors is harmonious and less concentrated, while in the difficult aspects (opposition, square, semisquare, sesquiquadrate) the working is disharmonious and less concentrated. Beginners should first learn the meanings for the aspects of conjunction, which can then be modified for the easy and difficult aspects involving the same planets.

The aspects for the Descendant, Lower Midheaven, and South Node are derived by taking the similar aspects under, respectively, the Ascendant, Midheaven, and North Node, and modifying them according to the key meanings of the Descendant, Lower Midheaven, and South Node.

For example, Mercury in difficult aspect with the North Node signifies manipulation of others, fraud, and a lack of inventiveness; but Mercury in difficult aspect with the South Node suggests hidden selfish motives, mental dullness or stupidity, the impulse to steal from others, and a lack of conscious self-control, because the key meaning of the South Node is taking, repression, concealing, and bad fortune. Of course, these two sets of meanings are in accord with each other, since the nodes of the Moon always act in unison, the North (ascending) Node giving and the South (descending) Node taking.

Sun Aspects

Planets aspected by the Sun will be vitalized and strengthened, and their actions will be united with that of the Sun. They will play an important role in the overall integration of forces that determines the character of the chart, or the person for whom the reading is done.

Sun-Ascendant
Conjunction: Forceful personality; cheerful, extroverted expression; need for recognition; love of the limelight
Easy: Achievement of ambitions; popularity; personal charm; ability to win others over
Difficult: Over-confidence, brashness; pushing too hard; unpleasantly aggressive personality

Sun-Midheaven
Conjunction: Goal-orientated; self-confidence; awareness of purpose; stable sense of identity
Easy: Well-adjusted life; happy with career and choices; earned success; positive attitude
Difficult: Unrealistic goals; lack of clear direction; shifting purposes; unstable sense of self

Sun-Moon
Conjunction: Strong emotions and instincts; obsession with self; creativity; cyclic physical disorders; entrenched habits
Easy: Harmonious home; good relations with parents, spouse; strong constitution; well-adjusted

Difficult: Divided purposes; dual nature; parental split; chronic disorders; excess of ambition; precocious genius

Sun-Mercury

Conjunction: Strong mental abilities; aptitude for learning; witty and expressive personality

Easy: Scholarship; literary or scientific achievement; ability to invent and innovate

Difficult: Self-centered attitude; imbalance of talents and skills; nervous and unsettled nature; susceptibility to stroke, seizure, or brainstorm

Sun-Venus

Conjunction: Expression of self through feelings; need to form close emotional ties; love of beauty and art; striving for intimacy and affection

Easy: Love of peace and ease; contentment in easy, loving surroundings; gentle soul.

Difficult: Irresponsibility; laziness; flight from harsh realities; soft body and weak mind

Sun-Mars

Conjunction: Attraction to danger; fiercely competitive; robust constitution; strong will; physical and mental endurance; decision-making powers

Easy: Positions of authority and leadership; heroic actions; strong moral stands

Difficult: Constantly picking disputes to test courage; quarrelsome nature; reckless overconfidence

Sun-Jupiter

Conjunction: Expansive and generous nature; love of justice; good fortune; noble purposes

Easy: Advancement and honors; opportunities for growth and expansion; recognition for talents and abilities

Difficult: Conflict with authorities; extravagant and pretentious behavior; obesity; liver trouble; conceited

Sun-Saturn

Conjunction: Awareness of self-limitation; disciplined behavior; self-consciousness results in hesitation and worry; pragmatic outlook

Easy: Patience to work within personal limits; hardship brings wisdom; reliability; slow but steady progress

Difficult: Possibly abusive father; inferiority complex; negative, self-pitying, selfish nature; poor health

Sun-North Node

Conjunction: Tendency to get own way; life proceeds as planned; doors are opened when opportunity knocks; fortunate birth circumstances

Easy: Advancement of purpose; cooperation of others; arguments prevail; heart's desire attained

Difficult: Willful and spoiled behavior; expectation of success without effort; lack of concentration or drive

Moon Aspects

The Moon receives the influence of planets aspected with it, and causes their action to be fluctuating and changeable in the area of personal instincts and emotional responses, and in the formation of habits and mannerisms.

Moon-Ascendant

Conjunction: Subjective, emotional attitude; impulse to be mothering or helpful; changeable, moody nature; habits easily formed

Easy: Responsive and adaptive to circumstances; perceptive of the desires and needs of others; feminine

Difficult: Hypersensitive and over-reactive; easily hurt or angered; trouble getting along with women; bad habits

Moon-Midheaven

Conjunction: Mother a strong formative influence; essential nature loving and sensitive; deep intuitive understanding

Easy: Ability to express emotions truly; innate talent for comforting and counseling others; home-loving

Difficult: Emotional injury caused by a woman; feelings get in the way of work; inconsistent; unreliable

Moon-Mercury

Conjunction: Quick, perceptive mind; good memory; natural wit; a way with words; born story-teller; active intellect; strong curiosity

Easy: Linguistic talent; feelings and emotions in harmony; love of poetry and song; healthy mental activity

Difficult: Too clever for own good; wit frequently misunderstood; sarcastic; erratic mind; loves change for its own sake

Moon-Venus

Conjunction: Romantic nature; makes friends easily and is popular; balanced outlook; charming personal manner

Easy: Musical; artistic talent; displays excellent personal taste and fashion sense; a fulfilling emotional life

Difficult: Trouble expressing feelings; slovenly or outrageous style of dress; longing for love; immoral behavior

Moon-Mars

Conjunction: Swift and forceful responses; emotions easily roused to boiling point; strong passions; very decided likes and dislikes; impetuous

Easy: Boldness and strong will; unpretentious and direct; self-controlled; speaks with candor.

Difficult: Judges others harshly; violent reactions; temper tantrums; rebels against authority; rash

Moon-Jupiter

Conjunction: Expansive, generous nature; loves to include others and share happiness; humanitarian impulses; hates to see suffering

Easy: Charitable giving of time and money; loved and respected; sound judgment; truthful and just

Difficult: Extravagant; carelessness leads to legal problems; poor judgment; well-meaning but negligent

Moon-Saturn

Conjunction: Cautious and conscientious manner; feelings of inadequacy; repressed emotions; moods oscillate between determination and despair

Easy: Self-control; work habits carry through phases of depression; duty to others more important than personal feelings

Difficult: Anxiety and hopelessness alternate; inability to find peace or contentment; painful self-consciousness; frigidity

Moon-North Node

Conjunction: Mother love; friends and family supportive and giving; nurturing environment; emotional needs met; fortunate in dealings with women

Easy: Devoted lover; true friends; happy unions; relationships based on strong affection; good relationship with mother

Difficult: Strained relationships; excess of nervous emotion; love of another smothers and oppresses; clinging friends and relations

Mercury Aspects

Mercury is neutral and lends its principle of communication and coordination to whichever planet it aspects, taking its direction and type of expression from the nature of that planet.

Mercury-Ascendant

Conjunction: Restless, inquiring personality; loves conversation and society of others; filled with bright nervous energy; eloquent and charming

Easy: Diplomatic and persuasive; sportive delight in debate; convincing; need to share ideas; many acquaintances

Difficult: Garrulous; likely to give offense through choice of words; argumentative; excitable; gossiping

Mercury-Midheaven

Conjunction: Love of knowledge; strong intellect; profession involved with teaching or learning; studious; thoughtful; need to express opinions and beliefs to others

Easy: Advancement in profession through social contacts; clarity of purpose; life is planned out; articulation of self image

Difficult: Vain about mental prowess; closed mind; shifting purposes; lack of objectivity; sophistry and empty rhetoric

Mercury-Venus

Conjunction: Charming and pleasant; artistic friends; loves theater, opera; refined manners; conscious of diction and grammar; love of words

Easy: Entertaining; witty; raconteur; life of the party; esthetic sense expresses itself in decor, clothing

Difficult: Social butterfly; demands attention and approval; ostentatious lifestyle; flirtatious

Mercury-Mars

Conjunction: Forceful in debate; direct, penetrating arguments; use of logic and factual data; physically energetic; fast reflexes; takes control of conversation

Easy: Many practical and useful suggestions; mental enterprise; brings ideas to reality; sharp physical senses

Difficult: Stress or breakdown through overwork; excess of deep thinking; snappish and irritable; critical and carping attitude; theft of ideas

Mercury-Jupiter

Conjunction: Broad-minded, generous attitude; ability to see the big picture; many creative ideas matched with strong judgment; philosophical temperament

Easy: Good business sense; talent for building organizations; cheerful, positive life attitude; depth of knowledge

Difficult: Poor judgment; reach exceeds grasp; business failure; overextended resources; excessive promotion; expansion too rapid

Mercury-Saturn

Conjunction: Logical but sterile mind; narrow concentration; hesitation to express thoughts and feelings openly; pragmatic and enduring; appears duller than is really the case

Easy: Methodical and calculating; builds assets by slow accumulation; aptitude for science involving repeated testing; organized; serious

Difficult: Rigid one-track mind; awkward and slow speech; sense of humor suppressed or hidden; unhappy; frugal; uncommunicative

Mercury-North Node

Conjunction: Increase of knowledge; profitable communications; pleasure in the company of others; fortunate relationships; joint interests prosper

Easy: Social ties bring good fortune; employment opportunity in field of communication; writings popular; happy expression of ideas

Difficult: Attempts to manipulate others; using friends; ideas slow to bear fruit; fraud; confidence artist

Venus Aspects

Planets aspected to Venus will be softened in their effects and brought into harmony. They will act upon the emotions and affection and modify the ability to form intimate relationships of a happy nature.

Venus-Ascendant

Conjunction: Affectionate and friendly nature; grace and physical beauty; love of adornment; well-mannered; affluent circumstances

Easy: Sympathetic and warm; kind; helpful; tactful; tendency to form love relationships; hospitality

Difficult: Poor choice of lovers; pleasure-loving nature; self-indulgent; straining to impress others with style of dress or possessions

Venus-Midheaven

Conjunction: Artistic, expressive nature; beautiful and graceful soul; abhorrence of anything cheap or ugly; natural rapport with women

Easy: Artistic profession; attractive manner draws others; an enduring love; true friends; contentment

Difficult: Vanity and self-satisfied manner alienate others; conflicts with women; superficial; jealous; conceited

Venus-Mars

Conjunction: Passionate sexual nature; attraction to the sensual and erotic; easily aroused to desire; physical lovemaking; magnetic; impulsive

Easy: Healthy sexuality; many lovers; ardent need to touch and arouse; creative expression

Difficult: Imprudent desires; compulsive sexual behavior; infidelity; easily infatuated; sexual diseases

Venus-Jupiter

Conjunction: Expansive, loving nature attracts numerous admirers; harmonious relations with others; wide social circle; works well with others

Easy: Glamorous lifestyle; public acclaim; skill at entertaining; hosting social events; enjoys nightlife

Difficult: Excessive indulgence in partying; unbalanced emotions; inability to be alone; excesses injure health

Venus-Saturn

Conjunction: Dutiful affections; expression of love limited; emotional coolness; older love partner; repressed affections; happiness in devotion

Easy: Sacrifice of pleasure for the happiness of others; loyal, sober, respectable nature; straightlaced; quiet fulfillment

Difficult: Prostitution of emotions; cold heart; exploitative or unhappy love; demanding and selfish; sad

Venus-North Node

Conjunction: Spontaneous friendships; charitable impulses; acts of kindness; expressions of affection; opening of the heart

Easy: Ability to please; beautiful creations; artistic expression; marriage proposals; declarations of love

Difficult: Unstable and short-lived relationships; creative dry spell; alternate giving and withholding of affection; separations

Mars Aspects

Planets aspected with Mars will be strongly reinforced, and will modify the passionate and energetic expression of emotion.

Mars-Ascendant

Conjunction: Strong will; assertive, aggressive attitude; need to dominate; courage; combative nature; forceful advancement

Easy: Leadership qualities; capacity for hard work; willingness to overcome hardship

Difficult: Aggressive and abusive; bullying tendencies; contentious; barbaric; indifferent to the feelings of others

Mars-Midheaven

Conjunction: Active, challenging profession; ambitious; independent; determined to achieve objectives; goal-orientated

Easy: Businesslike, no-nonsense attitude; efficient organizer; direct; forthright; climbing the corporate ladder

Difficult: Hasty decisions; fiery temper; conflict with superiors; loss of position; impulsive actions

Mars-Jupiter

Conjunction: Capacity for daring, difficult actions; physical strength and quickness; great courage; boldness; pleasure in testing personal limits

Easy: Zest for life; enterprising spirit; love of contact team sports; buoyant optimism; mischievous

Difficult: Extremist beliefs; impatience with system; rebellion against authority; superiority complex

Mars-Saturn

Conjunction: Disciplined body; controlled emotions; fitness fanatic; spartan lifestyle; tendency to be accident-prone

Easy: Endurance; tenacity; ability to withstand hardship and deprivation; self-reliant; enterprising

Difficult: Accidents due to rashness; harsh manner; violence; cruelty; stern attitude to life; physical strain

Mars-North Node

Conjunction: Gain through risk-taking; courageous actions; military honors; medals for heroism; women impressed by physical prowess; unexpected victory

Easy: Team victory in business or sports; loyalty; promotion in the military; boldness wins admiration

Difficult: Quarreling delays success; unexpected setbacks; disputes over who is in charge; dissidence hinders progress

Jupiter Aspects

Planets aspected with Jupiter have their actions made more fortunate and broadened in scope. They affect the expansive and cheerful impulse in human nature and the urge for personal growth through material acquisition and increased understanding.

Jupiter-Ascendant

Conjunction: Generous and charming manner; love of luxury and lavish surroundings; tendency to obesity; good-humored; attraction to nobility and those with wealth

Easy: Jovial; agreeable; popular disposition; well-liked; respected; seeks a rich environment

Difficult: Vain display of wealth; name-dropping; boastfulness; extravagant, wasteful lifestyle

Jupiter-Midheaven

Conjunction: Wealth; success; attainment of an easy and luxurious life; good fortune; born into rich family; natural nobility

Easy: Success with harmony; sense of belonging; humane; generous; civilized; judicial role

Difficult: Conditions unstable; risk of losing place; drop in social standing; desire to be seen as more important than is the case

Jupiter-Saturn

Conjunction: Optimism alternates with depression; need to seize opportunities when they arise; fallow periods; taking the long view brings expansion

Easy: Excellent business sense; aptitude for the stock market; strong sense of duty; honorable; religious or moral nature

Difficult: Dissatisfaction; inability to accept personal limitations; foolish optimism; unbalanced efforts

Jupiter-North Node

Conjunction: Extreme good fortune; all attempts succeed; charmed life; generous gifts; sharing of wealth; to the manor born; well-loved ruler or authority figure

Easy: Orderly, successful career; harmonious and profitable enterprise; happy marriage; good fellowship

Difficult: Minor losses; setbacks; unsettled social relations; authority questioned; unfounded expectation of success

Saturn Aspects

Planets in aspect with Saturn will have their actions limited and regulated. They will affect the personal ambitions in relation to the sense of inadequacy and self-consciousness.

Saturn-Ascendant

Conjunction: Inhibited expression; cautious, self-limiting attitude; shyness; frustration born of inability to express needs; harsh childhood

Easy: Experienced in life; reserved and serious manner; no illusions; faces reality squarely; attraction to older friends

Difficult: Cynical; broken by early abuse; alienated; fearful; lonely; cold environment

Saturn-Midheaven

Conjunction: Single-minded in pursuit of ambition; hard-working; stoic and uncommunicative; must strive to overcome many difficulties; slow advancement

Easy: Patient self-control in pursuit of goals; dependable; consistent; help from older individual; willingness to take on tedious hard work

Difficult: Self-doubt brings periods of despair; selfish and self-absorbed nature; pessimism; failure of hopes

Saturn-North Node

Conjunction: Others unsympathetic; gifts and honors given grudgingly or withheld; recognition delayed; antisocial nature creates negative climate; dislike of others

Easy: Supportive relationship with father figure; attains experience and wisdom; aptitude for recondite or occult subjects

Difficult: Loss of hope; withdrawal from the world; despair; suicidal thoughts; bitter disappointment

Ascending Node Aspects

Planets in aspect with the North Node will be made fortunate and giving and tend to elevate into conscious awareness. They will affect deliberate, clearly willed actions of generosity and honoring.

North Node-Ascendant

Conjunction: Generous, charitable attitude; unselfishness; fortunate in life; ability to charm and please others; physically attractive, talented; gifted with social grace

Easy: Sharing of time and energy; sociable, humane; work for the greater good; at ease in the public eye

Difficult: Dislike of solitude; expects too much from others; lack of generosity; puts self first; cannot maintain relationships

North Node-Midheaven

Conjunction: Conscious of own good fortune; sense of responsibility to share gifts, possessions with less fortunate; altruistic; a true and generous friend

Easy: Charitable work; missionary work; devotion to generous ideals; battles against inequity

Difficult: Misguided generosity; exploitation of others; partiality or bias; withholding of help to achieve own purposes

The Quine Runes

The runes that rule the seventy-two quines of the zodiac are interpreted with different shades of meaning that depend upon which planet, angle, or node occupies the quine. The influence of these quine runes upon the planets is modified by the aspects of each planet, the card rune that selects the sign of the planet, and whether the influence of the card rune upon the quine rune is direct or indirect.

You will remember that the rune on the card of each planet identifies which zodiac sign the planet shall occupy. A roll of the elemental die of that sign locates the specific quine of the planet, and in the process, one of the two quindecan runes in that sign is selected—either the same rune that is on the card of that planet, or its pair rune in the sign. When the quindecan that holds the quine of the planet in a sign has the same rune as that on the card of the planet, the influence of the card rune on the quine rune is direct.

Card runes exert the greatest influence upon the signs they occupy. Quindecan runes, which result from the relationship between card and die runes, exert their primary influence upon the houses holding them. A quindecan rune is said to occupy a house when the cusp, or first degree, of that house falls within the quindecan ruled by the rune. For example, if the cusp of the 7th house fell on the final quine of Capricorn (cusps are always located on the first degree of quines), the quindecan rune Othila (ᛟ) would occupy the 7th house even though two-thirds of its quindecan lay within the 6th house.

Below is a table of keywords that relates each of the Germanic runes to the Ascendant, Midheaven, planets, ascending node of the Moon, and twelve houses of the zodiac. Needless to say, a single word is insufficient to give the complete meaning of this relationship, but a larger understanding can be gained by comparing each word first horizontally with the other keywords of its rune, and then vertically with the other keywords of its planet or house.

Many other keywords might have been selected. The ones in this table should not be regarded as definitive, but treated as a quick guide and a prompt to the memory, and used as a basic foundation upon which to build a more complete understanding of the astrological relationships of the runes.

Runes	Ascendant	Midheaven	Sun	Moon
ᚠ	Acquisitive	Subservient	Wealthy	Dependant
ᚢ	Forceful	Dominating	Virile	Excitable
ᚦ	Insulting	Malicious	Contemptuous	Tormenting
ᚠ	Helpful	Benevolent	Persuasive	Sensitive
ᚱ	Searching	Hopeful	Questing	Wandering
ᚲ	Guiding	Promising	Constant	Vacillating
ᚷ	Giving	Sacrificing	Radiating	Receiving
ᚹ	Attaining	Rejoicing	Ecstatic	Cherishing
ᚺ	Destructive	Violent	Withering	Chaotic
ᚾ	Tormented	Deprived	Arid	Unrequited
ᛁ	Deceiving	Concealing	Superficial	Unresponsive
ᛋ	Altering	Changing	Improving	Reforming
ᛃ	Reliable	Steadfast	Strong	Nurturing
ᛈ	Indulgent	Enjoying	Opulent	Decadent
ᛉ	Protecting	Warning	Shielding	Defensive
ᛊ	Active	Vitalizing	Blasting	Punishing
ᛏ	Equitable	Honorable	Heroic	Compromising
ᛒ	Conceiving	Fertile	Devoted	Receptive
ᛗ	Advancing	Resourceful	Progressive	Habitual
ᛙ	Inventive	Creative	Inspired	Reflective
ᛚ	Receptive	Intuitive	Artistic	Mediumistic
◇	Producing	Growing	Evolving	Domestic
ᛝ	Completing	Fulfilling	Revealing	Veiling
ᛜ	Distinguishing	Identifying	Cosmopolitan	Clannish

Runes	Mercury	Venus	Mars	Jupiter
ᚠ	Commercial	Gentle	Timid	Productive
ᚢ	Voluble	Passionate	Aggressive	Enterprising
ᚦ	Profane	Perverse	Cruel	Abusive
ᚨ	Eloquent	Supportive	Forthright	Instructive
ᚱ	Curious	Yearning	Restless	Outgoing
ᚲ	Exposing	Satisfying	Focused	Leading
ᚷ	Explaining	Adoring	Imprudent	Lavish
ᚹ	Understanding	Displaying	Glorying	Celebrating
ᚺ	Blustering	Impulsive	Furious	Explosive
ᚾ	Inarticulate	Loveless	Consuming	Emaciated
ᛁ	Prevaricating	Frigid	Heartless	Delaying
ᛇ	Hypocritical	Blooming	Vindictive	Profiting
ᛃ	Factual	Constant	Tough	Serviceable
ᛈ	Poetic	Sensual	Excessive	Extravagant
ᛉ	Forbidding	Possessive	Threatening	Expelling
ᛋ	Incisive	Heartbroken	Attacking	Executing
ᛏ	Truthful	Faithful	Courageous	Adventurous
ᛒ	Flattering	Amorous	Lustful	Pregnant
ᛗ	Literal	Graceful	Conquering	Constructing
ᛞ	Rational	Charming	Ruling	Governing
ᛚ	Imaginative	Romantic	Obsessive	Creative
ᛜ	Original	Virtuous	Guarding	Nourishing
ᛟ	Expressive	Demonstrative	Enforcing	Presenting
ᛝ	Patriotic	Loyal	Proud	Expansionary

Runes	Saturn	Dragon's Head	1st House	2nd House
ᛤ	Conservative	Profiting	Body	Money
ᚢ	Selfish	Imposing	Potency	Greed
ᚦ	Withholding	Poisonous	Defamation	Vandalism
ᚠ	Critical	Illuminating	Self-expression	Brokerage
ᚱ	Discontent	Pursuing	Urges	Vehicle
ᚲ	Receding	Realizing	Goals	Prizes
ᚷ	Ungenerous	Endowed	Ability	Gifts
ᚹ	Unsatisfied	Exalted	Satisfaction	Rewards
ᚺ	Treacherous	Uncontrolled	Hostility	Damage
ᛏ	Neglected	Needy	Needs	Theft
ᛁ	Frozen	Evasive	Self-deception	Fraud
ᛃ	Disappointed	Lucky	Transformation	Exchange
ᛇ	Inflexible	Useful	Steadfastness	Maintenance
ᛈ	Perverse	Surfeited	Pleasures	Luxuries
ᛉ	Repelling	Refusing	Self-defense	Security
ᛊ	Wrathful	Repaying	Vitality	Strength
ᛏ	Hesitant	Upholding	Honor	Pride
ᛒ	Impotent	Germinating	Fertility	Acquisition
ᛗ	Sickly	Skillful	Skills	Valuables
ᛘ	Practical	Gifted	Intellect	Vanity
ᛚ	Melancholic	Visionary	Unconscious	Fears
◇	Dutiful	Fruitful	Growth	Possessions
ᛝ	Defining	Fulfilling	Lifespan	Common sense
ᛟ	Prejudiced	Hospitable	Identity	Collections

Runes	3rd House	4th House	5th House	6th House
ᚠ	Associations	Pets	Fitness	Disease
ᚢ	Assertiveness	Possessiveness	Sports	Hardiness
ᚦ	Gossip	Cruelty	Testing	Criticism
ᚨ	Advice	Mother	Father	Counselor
ᚱ	Visiting	Homesickness	Challenges	Integration
ᚲ	Friends	Home	Achievements	Wholesomeness
ᚷ	Compliments	Tenderness	Risk	Service
ᚹ	Acceptance	Gratitude	Honors	Contentment
ᚺ	Spite	Abuse	Recklessness	Intolerance
ᚾ	Ostracism	Neglect	Injury	Imbalance
ᛁ	Disinformation	Withdrawal	Inaction	Isolation
ᛃ	Socializing	Moving	Recovery	Reintegration
ᛇ	True-blue	Homemaking	Reliability	Fidelity
ᛈ	Novelty	Holidays	Playfulness	Immodesty
ᛉ	Unfashionable	Protectiveness	Precautions	Disinfecting
ᛋ	Style	Advocacy	Masterstroke	Purging
ᛏ	Truth	Respect	Magnanimity	Arrogance
ᛒ	Meeting	Pregnancy	Children	Inhibitions
ᛗ	Etiquette	Growth	Practice	Efficiency
ᛘ	Charm	Nurturing	Talents	Discipline
ᛚ	Doubts	Habits	Creations	Suppressing
ᛜ	Siblings	Family	Fruitfulness	Conformity
ᛝ	Culture	Independence	Achievements	Dedication
ᛟ	Experiences	Property	Home field	Community

Runes	7th House	8th House	9th House	10th House
ᚡ	Attraction	Submission	Travel	Investment
ᚢ	Passion	Dominance	Restlessness	Speculating
ᚦ	Adultery	Malice	Cynicism	Back-stabbing
ᚠ	Lawyer	Executor	Teacher	Praise
ᚱ	Unrequitedness	Pursuit	Quest	Competing
ᚲ	Union	Desire	Guide	Advancement
ᚷ	Devotion	Sacrifice	Study	Toil
ᚹ	Love	Rebirth	Knowledge	Achievement
ᚺ	Quarrels	Spirit possession	Dislocation	Frustration
ᚾ	Rejection	Assault	Confinement	Obligations
ᛁ	Betrayal	Grave	Stagnation	Misrepresenting
ᛇ	Transition	Inheritance	Re-emergence	Promotion
ᛃ	Constancy	Brutality	Perseverance	Construction
ᛈ	Lovemaking	Perversion	Compensation	Status symbols
ᛉ	Jealousy	Rape	Delays	Setbacks
ᛋ	Exposure	Climax	Breakthrough	Willpower
ᛏ	Vows	Impregnation	Initiation	Contracts
ᛒ	Lover	Conception	Revelation	Ground-breaking
ᛗ	Adornment	Rituals	Intellect	Training
ᛙ	Beauty	Mysticism	Curiosity	Enterprise
ᛚ	Glamour	Obsessions	Dreams	Visionary
◇	Marriage	Fruition	Prophecy	Production
ᛟ	Anniversaries	Regeneration	Writings	Career
ᛜ	Partnership	Death	Philosophy	Business

Runes	11th House	12th House
ᚠ	Groups	Ill health
ᚢ	Joining	Enduring
ᚦ	Emotionalism	Self-pity
ᚨ	Reason	Ministering
ᚱ	Interests	Hopes
ᚲ	Conclusions	Ideals
ᚷ	Analysis	Offerings
ᚹ	Insight	Ecstasy
ᚺ	Arguments	Self-dissatisfaction
ᛏ	Doubt	Loneliness
ᛁ	Hypocrisy	Solitude
ᛋ	Reassessment	Release
ᛁ	Commitment	Self-abnegation
ᛐ	Dilettantism	Fantasies
ᛉ	Advocacy	Withdrawal
ᛋ	Disillusion	Calling
ᛏ	Accuracy	Duty
ᛒ	Enthusiasm	Direction
ᛗ	Experiments	Tranquility
ᛘ	Judgments	Meditation
ᛚ	Utopianism	Memories
◊	Politics	Occultism
ᛡ	Phase	Reincarnation
ᛜ	Reformism	Faith

Interpreting the Chart

Interpreting the runic astrology oracle presents many of the same problems to the beginner as those found in reading a regular horoscope. There is confusion and doubt about how to begin, and what should be looked at first. Even when the various meanings of the individual runes and planets in their signs and houses are collected together, it is difficult to know how to synthesize these bits and pieces into a smooth, meaningful whole.

Everyone who uses the oracle will develop their own personal approach. In time a degree of ease will be attained that will allow the diviner to give a preliminary reading in the presence of the querent even as the counters of the planets are placed upon the large chart. Experienced astrologers should face little difficulty in incorporating the rune meanings into the astrological context, and will find that the runes illuminate questions that might otherwise remain obscure. For those with no practice in astrology, the following step by step approach to interpreting the oracle may prove useful as a way of gaining familiarity with it.

As you proceed through the steps, make a written record of your understanding of the meaning of each relationship using as much detail as you feel necessary to record all vital information. The oracle will unfold itself in your awareness as you examine it. A complete analysis may take several days for a beginner due to the need to go back and look up the meanings of different aspects and other relationships. With familiarity you will find yourself grasping the essence of the oracle almost before you have had time to lay it out.

Step One

Look first to the Significator rune. The Significator is to the runes what the Ascendant is to the horoscope. It acts as a benchmark to the interpretation. Whenever there is difficulty in understanding any part of the chart, runic or astrological, relate it back to the Significator. It is very promising if this rune is of a beneficent type, but even if the rune seems malefic it may be possible to turn its violent or hurtful elements to good use and release their energy in controlled, constructive ways.

Step Two

Examine the chart for any overall pattern assumed by the planets. The locations of the Ascendant, Midheaven, and lunar nodes are usually not considered when defining these patterns, which fall into seven generally recognized types, first described by the American astrologer Marc Edmund Jones:[1]

1) *Splash pattern:* a wide and even scattering of the planets around the zodiac with no discernable focus, suggesting a broad interest in many ideas and divergent cultures and a tolerance for the unusual; but negatively, a lack of direction and purpose.

2) *Bundle pattern:* all planets fall upon one-third of the circle of the signs, the remaining two-thirds empty, indicating a narrow life limited by circumstances and an inhibited character.

3) *Locomotive pattern:* the planets are lined up in a "train" that curves around two-thirds of the zodiac, leaving the remaining third empty. The planet leading the train in a counterclockwise direction is dominant, and the empty third of the chart usually indicates a weakness in the personality.

4) *Bowl pattern:* all planets occupy one half of the zodiac. When they fall into one of the four hemispheres, its nature can provide a clue to the chart. A self-contained, withholding personality presenting one area of experience to the world while being excluded or divided from another.

5) *Bucket pattern:* same as the bowl but with a single planet in the opposite half circle of the zodiac, representing the handle of the bucket, which acts as the outlet of communication for all the other planetary principles. The expression is strengthened if the solitary planet is alone in one of the four hemispheres.

A variation on the bucket pattern is what is known as the *sling pattern,* in which all planets occupy one-third of the chart except one, which is opposite them and acts as a focus for their energies, resulting in a very concentrated, forceful individual with a definite and narrow interest.

6) *See-saw pattern:* planets form two groups opposite each other across the center of the chart, resulting in a constant awareness of opposing viewpoints and a sensitivity and responsiveness to alternate possibilities, with the potential power that always results from conditions of high tension.

7) *Splay pattern:* planets occur clumped in irregularly spaced groups around the chart, indicating a forceful and bold personality that defies convention and always seeks to fulfill its own aspirations.

To these recognized types might be added two more I have noticed in my own work, which do not fit comfortably into any of the above types:

8) *Triangle pattern:* the planets are arranged in three groups that form the points of a triangle of roughly equal sides, indicating a general harmony and order in the chart, even where the trine aspects formed between individual planets are not always perfect. If each point of the triangle falls predominantly within one sign, one of the four elements will dominate.

9) *Cross pattern:* the planets are arranged on four corners of the zodiac, indicating a general tension and disorder in the chart even when the square aspects between individual planets are not always perfect. If each arm of the cross falls predominantly within one sign, one of the three qualities will dominate.

Step Three

After examining the general pattern, look for specific compound aspects such as the grand trine, grand cross, and T-square. Then take note of any especially strong group of planets, and pick out the individual planets that stand apart from the rest due to the strength of their position and aspects. Notice planets located in conjunction with, or very near, the angles of the Ascendant, Midheaven, Descendant, and Lower Midheaven, as these angles will influence their function.

Record the number of planets that occupy positive signs and those that fall into negative signs, omitting from consideration the nodes of the Moon; include, however, the points of the Ascendant and Midheaven, which lie in signs at a right angle to each other and are always of opposite polarity. An excess of positive signs shows expressiveness and spontaneity; an excess of negatives shows repression and passivity.

Make the same numerical division of the planets, plus the Ascendant and Midheaven, minus the nodes, into the three quadruplicities of cardinal, fixed, and mutable qualities. A larger number of cardinal planets indicates enterprise and drive; more fixed shows intensity and steadfastness; more mutable, adaptability and variability.

Make a third division of the number of planets and points of Ascendant and Midheaven that occupy the triplicities of the four elements fire, water, air, and earth. A larger number of planets in fire signs reveals energy and assertion in the chart; more in water means emotion and intuition; more in air, mental agility and communication; more in earth, practicality and restraint.

Step Four

Look at the nine card runes that located the planets, plus the points of the Ascendant and North Node, on the chart. Note how many fall into the Fehu aett, how many are of the Hagalaz aett, and how many are of the Teiwaz aett. A majority in the family of Fehu suggests a material or health slant to the reading; a majority in the Hagalaz family indicates a predominance of emotional factors and personal inter-relationships; a majority in the Teiwaz family indicates an intellectual or spiritual slant.

Step Five

Begin a detailed analysis of the chart by noting the sign that holds the quine of the Ascendant. Relate this to the sign and house occupied by the natural ruler of the Ascendant sign—for example, if the Ascendant is in Taurus, take note which sign and house holds Venus, because Venus rules Taurus. There is a sympathetic connection between the sign on the Ascendant and the sign and house that hold its ruler, and by comparing them together very important leading information can often be gathered that illuminates other areas of the chart. Briefly write down your understanding of this relationship.

Record and explain aspects formed by the planets with the Ascendant degree. In marking aspects on the small chart it is useful to draw the difficult aspects with red ink and the easy aspects with blue ink. It is not the usual practice in astrology, but I mark down the aspects of the Ascendant and Midheaven as well as the aspects of the nodes of the Moon. These are as a general rule omitted from the chart. I find it useful to include them because it provides a constant visual reminder of the influence of these points. Of course the lunar nodes are invariably in opposition to each other.

Next in importance after the Ascendant is the position of the Sun. Make notes on the sign and house it occupies, then consider the Sun ruler, which is the planet that rules the sign occupied by the Sun. The Sun and the Sun ruler have a sympathetic relationship and should be considered together for meaning, even though they may not be in aspect. Analyze any aspects formed by the Sun with the other planets. Do the same for the Moon.

The Sun and Moon are called the greater and lesser lights of the heavens, and with the Ascendant are the most important indicators in the chart. The astrologer Jeff Mayo has gone so far as to assert that a true assessment of a person's character can be derived from these three factors alone, considering only the signs they occupy.[2]

Analyze the positions by sign and house and the aspects formed with the other planets, taking notes as you go, in the following order: Mercury, Venus, Mars, Jupiter, Saturn. You will find as you come to the outer planets that you have already considered most of their aspects earlier in their relation to the Ascendant, Sun, Moon, and inner planets. Finally, give thought to the significance of the nodes of the Moon, observing the signs and houses they occupy and the planets they aspect.

The aspects of Midheaven will automatically be covered in this process of analysis. Many astrologers prefer to consider the lunar nodes first rather than last, but this makes little difference provided all factors of the chart are included in the final judgment.

Step Six

When you have looked at the astrological elements of the chart for their basic meanings, consider them in the same order with regard to the runes that locate and influence them. At first it will be useful to do this as a separate step. After you become familiar with using the oracle, you will begin to include this rune analysis for each planet automatically as you go from one to the other. The runes are of great help in clarifying meanings that at first glance may appear confusing or seem to make no sense.

There are three runes that influence each planet or significant point on the zodiac. The first is the card rune which locates the sign of the planet or point. This has the broadest influence of the three and extends across the entire 30 degrees of the sign it occupies. Apply the card rune to the sign that holds that card's planet.

The second rune is the rune that rules the quindecan of the sign it occupies in the zodiac. Each sign holds one pair of runes. Pair-runes have complementary meanings. Each planet will come under the influence of one of these quindecan runes, which acts as the connecting link between the card rune and the die rune. The quindecan rune is not directly selected, but results from the relationship between the card rune and the die rune.

The quindecan rune can be either the same as the card rune, or its paired complement in that sign. If it is the same, the influence of the planet upon the sign will be pure and unobstructed; if it is opposite, the influence of the planet on the sign will be modified according to the relationship that exists between the pair-runes in that sign. Apply the quindecan rune to the house that holds the planet under that quindecan.

The third rune influencing any planet is the die rune, which locates the planet in one of the six quines (divisions of 5 degrees) once its sign has been determined by the card rune. The die rune exerts a direct influence over the planet itself, and is related back to the card rune through the mediation of the quindecan rune. The die rune is a more directly focused active influence than the card rune, which functions as its passive backdrop.

When trying to establish the significance of a planet in a certain sign and house, consider these three runes as a connected series of meanings that bridge the gap between the astrological factors and tie them together.

Two planets may occupy the same sign, and when they do, they will have different card runes. Each card rune should be applied to the sign in considering the particular planet it locates. Remember, the card rune is not descriptive of the sign in isolation, but explains the sign in relation to the working of the planet it places on that sign. Therefore it is not contradictory to apply two card runes to one sign.

Because the South Node is located by the North Node, it does not possess a card rune. The same is true of the degree of Midheaven, which is located in the sign at a right angle clockwise from the Ascendant sign. To discover which pair-rune of the sign holding either of these points should be associated with that sign, take your cue from the card runes of the Ascendant and North Node.

If the card rune of the Ascendant is the same as the quindecan rune of its sign, make the rune influencing the sign of Midheaven also the same as its quindecan rune. On the other hand, if the card rune of the Ascendant is the pair-rune of the quindecan rune selected by the die toss for its sign, make the rune influencing the sign of Midheaven to be the pair-rune of its quindecan rune. Do the same in the case of the South Node relative to the North Node.

For example, if your card rune for the ascending node of the Moon is Sowelu (ϟ) and the die rune you cast for that sign also happens to be Sowelu, which places the ascending node under the quindecan of Algiz (Ϟ), then the card rune of the sign Virgo (ϟ) will be the pair-rune of the rune of the quindecan, (Υ). Therefore the rune of the opposite sign, Pisces, which joins that sign to the descending node of the Moon, and has the greatest influence over the sign, will be Jera ($\diamond$), the pair-rune of the rune of the quindecan containing the descending node. Of course, the quine rune of the descending node is Jera ($\diamond$) because it is 180 degrees opposite the quine rune of the ascending node.

To take a second example, if the Ascendant is located in Taurus by the card rune Gebo (X), and the die rune cast is Wunjo (P), the quindecan rune of the sign is the same as its card rune, because the quine rune occupies the quindecan of Gebo. Midheaven will fall 90° clockwise in Aquarius, on the quine of Kano ($\langle$). Taking the cue from the Ascendant, the card rune of Midheaven will be the same as its quindecan rune, Raido (R). Even though no card is dealt for the Midheaven degree, it should be assumed to have a card rune influencing its sign.

Step Seven

Look at the nine runes of the cards you laid out to locate the planets, angles, and lunar nodes, not in relation to those planets and the zodiac, but simply as runes in relation to each other. The runes are read left to right from the bottom row to the top row. A rune that comes after an earlier rune is based or founded upon that earlier rune and should be interpreted in conjunction with it.

The bottom row generally refers to the past circumstances, but these may be ongoing in the present as well and may have ramifications in the future. It is better to think of it as the base or foundation of the question the reading is concerned about. It should be read as an intelligible statement composed of symbolic indicators. The first rune on the left is the active agent, the second rune in the middle is the nature of the action, and the third rune on the right is the matter acted upon.

The middle row generally concerns the present state of affairs, but can also be thought of as the central focus of the question and the pivot it turns upon. Read the runes from left to right as another symbolic sentence that extends the information conveyed by the first sentence of symbols. The middle rune of the middle row is the central rune. All other runes are congruent to it and may be related back to this central rune for additional meaning.

The top row has to do with the future outcome or development of the matter under question, and may be looked upon as the state to which all previous indicators are leading. Read it left to right as a sentence conveying a single connected idea. Do not view it as inevitable and predestined; it is only an explanation of where past and present events are taking the matter, and may be regarded as a confirmation of hopeful expectations if it is favorable, or as a warning of possible trouble if it is unfavorable. It serves as a guideline for actions to improve the future.

Additional understanding can be gained from the runes by considering the columns separately. The left column reveals the primary influences that extend through the lifespan of the matter under consideration, the forces that move events. The middle column shows the actual manner in which these forces act and the nature of the evolution taking place. The right column indicates the matter upon which the motivational forces of the left column work.

Still more insight can be gained by considering the diagonals that cross through the heart of the runes. These represent opposing or conflicting influences that extend across the time span of the matter from past to future, with their focus in the present. Each diagonal is read from left to right as a symbolic statement. The upper-left to lower-right diagonal is unfavorable or obstructive; the lower-left to upper-right diagonal is favorable or constructive.

Step Eight

With the basic information you have gathered from the chart before you, it is time to select a set of categories through which you can apply it in an interpretive way to the actual subject matter of the reading. Categorizing the notes draws them together and unites them in an intelligible way, transforming them from a collection of unconnected associations into a unified analysis.

The categories you select will depend on the subject; a general life reading will have broader groupings than a reading directed to a specific time span or a narrow field of endeavor. For example, someone may wish to inquire into the circumstances and outcome of a contemplated surgery. This reading will receive a different emphasis than another which seeks insight about educational directions and future career options.

In considering each category, attention should usually focus first on the houses that relate to it, then on the signs of those houses and rulers of the signs. A house is related to a sign when the cusp of the house (its first degree) falls within the sign. Next look at the planets in these houses to judge how strong or weak they are, and at the aspects that affect them. Finally examine the runes involved.

1) *Character:* the general qualities and characteristics that make up an individual, or in the case of a reading concerned with a situation or event, the underlying conditions that act as its foundation.

Consult the Sun and Sun ruler (planet ruling the sign occupied by the Sun), Moon, and Moon ruler; overall structure of the chart; dominant aspect patterns; significator rune.

2) *Personality:* the presentation of the self to the world, which is conditioned by the environment and is frequently mistaken for the true self, both by the individual wearing the mask and by others who look upon it.

Consult the Ascendant house (1st house), Ascendantruler (planet ruling the sign occupied by the Ascendant quine); planets in the ascending sign; aspects formed with the Ascendant quine.

3) *Identity:* the enduring light of consciousness that transcends temporary personal poses and is the essential truth of an individual's nature.

Consult Midheaven house (10th house), the Midheaven ruler (planet ruling sign occupied by Midheaven quine); planets in the sign at Midheaven; aspects to the Midheaven quine; Jupiter and Saturn (for patterns of mental development).

4) *Spiritual Level:* level of awareness that transcends logic and judgment, relying on insight and an inherent sense of truth or rightness. It concerns such matters as faith, religion, inspiration and occultism.

Consult the 8th (occultism), 9th (dreams, visions) and 12th (mediumship) houses; Jupiter and its aspects (higher consciousness); nodes of the Moon (conscious-unconscious duality); Lower Midheaven (hidden forces).

5) *Mental Level:* the level of reason, learning and study, the personal philosophy or view of the world, creativity and communication skills.

Consult the 3rd (communication); 5th (creativity) and 9th (study) houses; house and sign of Mercury and its aspects (art and science); Saturn and its aspects (philosophy).

6) *Emotional Level:* the level of feelings, likes and dislikes, the affections, attraction to or conflict with others, responses to sensations and emotions.

Consult the 3rd (casual reactions), 8th (sexual feelings), and 11th (interactions) houses; the water signs (emotional energy); Venus and its aspects (feelings and attractions); Moon and its aspects (emotional responses); Mars and its aspects (conflicts and sexual energies).

7) *Physical Level:* the level of health and disease, strength and weakness, vitality and endurance, appearance and general fitness.

Consult the 1st (general indicator), 6th (physical weaknesses), 7th (physical attractiveness), and 12th (chronic illness) houses; Sun (vitality and health of the heart); Moon (mental problems and complaints of women); Saturn (chills and falls); Mars (inflammations, burns, scalds, cuts and fever); Jupiter (liver trouble); any planet severely afflicted by its placement and aspects.

8) *Family:* concerns interpersonal relationships in the home environment involving parents, children, brothers and sisters.

Consult the 3rd (brothers and sisters), 4th (parents and the home), and 5th (children) houses; Moon (mother) and Sun (father); Mercury (brothers and sisters).

9) *Friends:* interpersonal relationships beyond the home environment involving associates, neighbors, acquaintances and personal ties.

Consult the 3rd (casual acquaintances) and 11th (friendships) houses; Venus (power to attract); Mars (power to reach out); Mercury (power to harmonize).

10) *Love:* strong and enduring interpersonal bonds such as those formed in love affairs or marriage.

Consult the 5th (love affairs and children) and 7th (marriage or common law relationships) houses; Moon in a man's chart; Sun in a woman's chart (opposite sex).

11) *Business:* the work of earning a living in pursuit of financial and material security through the career, financial matters and employments.

Consult the 6th (capacity for work), 7th (business partners), 8th and 2nd (money), and 10th (career) houses; Jupiter (opportunities to expand and establish new enterprises); Saturn (areas to conserve and approach with caution); Mars (bold initiatives).

12) *Recreation:* pursuits indulged in for pleasure and entertainment without a primary focus on a material return, such as sports, hobbies and other leisure activities.

Consult the 1st (interests and aptitudes) and 5th (pleasures) houses; Sun and Sun ruler; Moon and Moon ruler (general indicators); Mars (physical boldness and the taking of risks).

13) *Travel:* physical journeys beyond the everyday setting such as vacations, relocation, or business trips.

Consult the 3rd (short trips) and 9th (long trips) houses; the relationship between Mercury and Jupiter (wanderlust).

When these eight steps have been completed and the notes made during each step collected and considered together, a process of synthesis must take place that fuses the meanings of all the elements of the oracle into a single exposition of the subject of the divination. If the reading is done on the large chart in the presence of the querent, of course the preceding steps will be conducted mentally, and the exposition will be verbal. But if the reading is made over time using the small chart, write down your completed analysis and final conclusions in a concise but detailed essay.

The essay should be at least several pages in length, and may easily extend to ten pages or more, depending on the complexity of the question and the amount of information revealed by the oracle. Although the average person will not understand, and may not even be interested in, the rune and astrological relationships that went into the reading, it is a good idea to jot these down above the paragraph or beside the sentence in the analysis to which they apply, so that the reason for every conclusion is clearly set forth. The diviner must do this in any case on the copy of the reading he or she keeps for reference purposes, so that the chart will make sense if it is ever necessary to consider it in the distant future.

I like to present the querent with a report that contains both the pertinent categories selected from step eight above and the prose essay that summarizes my analysis of the reading. Others may wish to keep the categories as background information and give the querent only the final essay itself with the completed small chart. This is a matter of personal taste.

15

Sample Life Reading

The best way to learn runic astrology is to use it. Below is an in-depth life reading done by me during the long process of testing and evaluating the oracle. Refer to it as a practical example of procedure if you encounter any difficulty in understanding how to set up the runic astrology chart and do a reading. It illustrates the steps followed in interpreting the oracle, and shows how to accurately enter the necessary information as a permanent record on the small chart.

The following notes are written up at great length to show the process of analyzing a life chart in its entirety. In practice they would probably be much briefer. You would put down on paper only those relationships you need to prompt your memory and ensure that you do not omit important information in the finished written report that is presented to the querent along with a copy of the small chart.

There is no single, absolutely correct reading for any oracle. If you find that your interpretation of the following chart differs from my own, this does not necessarily mean that you are wrong, only that we viewed the same chart from different perspectives and each drew from its totality our own partial and individual understanding.

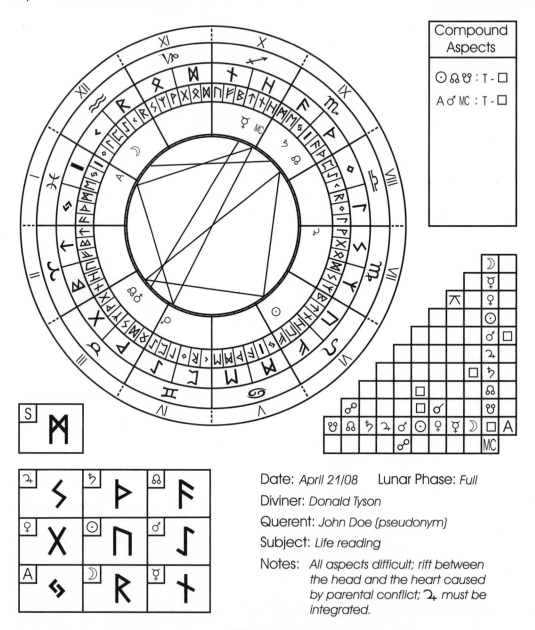

Compound
Aspects

☉ ☊ ☍ : T - □

A ♂ MC : T - □

S

Date: *April 21/08*   Lunar Phase: *Full*

Diviner: *Donald Tyson*

Querent: *John Doe (pseudonym)*

Subject: *Life reading*

Notes: *All aspects difficult; rift between
the head and the heart caused
by parental conflict; ♃ must be
integrated.*

Figure 15-1

Reading One

Querent: John Doe (pseudonym)

Subject: Life reading

John is in his mid-thirties and is struggling to make his living as a writer of science fiction. He also writes poetry. He is keenly interested in Eastern philosophy, mysticism and the occult. Single and withdrawn by nature, he lives at home with his mother. His father was an alcoholic who dies about fifteen years prior to the date of the reading. John says that his father was not abusive, but that he held expectations about his son that John found himself unable to fulfill, and to some extent John feels he let his father down because he could not be as aggressive and successful as his father wished. He has one older sister who was domineering and insensitive toward him during his childhood, and a younger brother with whom he feels quite close. Both siblings are married. John is not dating at the present time. He admits that relationships have always been difficult for him. Two primary goals occupy his energies: to achieve success in his literary work, and to attain a spiritual rebirth that will allow him to understand his purpose in life.

1) *Significator Rune: Mannaz* (ᛗ)

This is the rune for archetypal man, the Adam of the human race, the microcosm of the universe. It stands for the uniquely human powers of intellect and imagination, an awareness of a higher reality and the ability to dream. It also symbolizes the will and art of the magician to cause transformation both inwardly and outwardly. A very favorable rune.

2) *Overall Pattern: Splay; Cross*

The planets are clumped around the zodiac, indicating a selective and determined temperament that seizes upon certain aspects of experience and ignores or denies others. This results in a nature that is irregular and uneven in its response to life. The grouping of the planets is not random, but describes a rough cross, the arms of which lie on or near the fixed signs of the zodiac. One axis of the cross is the Sun-Moon near opposition; the other axis is the near opposition of Mars, Venus, and the South Node at Midheaven opposite Mercury, Saturn, and the North Node at Lower Midheaven. This suggests a fundamental division in the life between conscious and unconscious forces around the Sun-Moon axis.

3) *Astrological Groups*

Compound aspects—T-square: ☉ ☊ ☋

T-square: A ♂ MC

Conjunctions—♂ ☌ IC ; ♀ ☌ ☋

(All aspects are difficult—no easy aspects)

Outstanding planets—☉ ♌ (rules) ; ♀ ♉ (rules)

Polarity—Positive: 5 (MC ☉ ☽ ♀ ♂) ; Negative: 4 (A ♀ ♃ ♄)

Qualities—Cardinal: none

Fixed: 4 (☉ ☽ ♀ ♄)

Mutable: 5 (A ☿ ♂ ♃ MC)

Elements—Fire: 3 (☉ MC ☿)

Water: 2 (A ♄)

Air: 2 (☽ ♂)

Earth: 2 (♀ ♃)

4) *Rune Groups*

Families—Fehu: 5 (ᚱ ᚷ ᚺ ᚦ ᚠ)

Hagalaz: 4 (ᛉ ᛏ ᛃ ᛊ)

Teiwaz: none

Elements—Fire: 2 (ᛏ ᚺ)

Water: 3 (ᛉ ᚦ ᚠ)

Air: 2 (ᚱ ᛃ)

Earth: 2 (ᚷ ᛊ)

5) *Astrological Factors*

Ascendant: ♓

The mutable-water nature of this sign indicates strong emotions and intuitions coupled with the need to attain a distant ideal goal. Variability and hidden depths. Sudden unforeseen emotional storms, potent undercurrents. The dual nature of the higher and lower self pull in different directions. John is easily elated or depressed depending on the treatment he receives from others, because he takes the impression of his environment and reflects it. There is a tendency to avoid the harshness of the world by withdrawing from it. He is compassionate and sympathetic, very passive toward others and willing to follow their lead, at least outwardly. Creative, artistic, maybe psychic or mediumistic. He tends to be overemotional and indecisive.

Ascendant Ruler: ♃ ♍ in 7th

Jupiter, the life principle of expansion and growth, is in detriment in Virgo, indicating its hindrance due to an excessive self-criticism and a straining after an ideal of perfection. Its presence in the 7th house suggests that this self-critical attitude will inhibit John's ability to relate with others and coexist in unity and harmony with them. This is further reinforced by the fact that Jupiter is unaspected, and therefore cut off from the rest of the factors interacting to form John's life.

Ascendant Aspects: A □ (♂ ☍ IC)

Frustrated and suppressed self-assertion, with restricted activity and limited self-expression. Pent-up emotion, anger seething below the surface. Potential for violent outbursts.

Sun: ☉ ♌ in 6th

The Sun in its natural sign indicates that the principle of self-integration is a powerful factor in the chart, and can best express itself to reconcile contrary influences in the character through an energetic and assertive self-expression (♌) in the context of relationships with other people (7th), especially close relationships with the opposite sex. Sun ruler: Sun is in its natural sign.

Sun Aspects: ☉ □ ☊ ☋

The T-square relationship between the Sun and the lunar nodes emphasizes the need to integrate two opposing sides of the character, the emotional, loving side (♀ ♉), which is being neglected and suppressed (☋), with the critical, intellectual side (♄ ♐), which is the focus of the conscious attention (☊). It is as though the vital energy of the feelings, the need for love and tenderness, is being sucked out in a vampiric way to sustain the drive to study and analyze and understand.

Moon: ☽ ♒ in 12th

The Moon in Aquarius indicates that the mode of self-expression—behavior, mannerisms, habits—will be independent and detached, somewhat aloof and cool, with the main concern focused upon scientific or intellectual pursuits. Its location in the 12th house means that this coolness will manifest itself by a withdrawal from the world, with a fondness for solitude or a tendency to descend into the waters of the imagination.

It is impossible to consider the Moon in isolation from the Sun. These two lights of the heavens frequently stand for the mother and father. In John's chart they are almost in direct opposition in the fixed (i.e. entrenched) signs Aquarius (the head) and Leo (the heart). The Moon is in an airy sign, the Sun in a fiery sign—an explosive combination. All this strongly suggests an entrenched dispute, or an emotional rift, or an actual physical separation of his parents at an important formative time in John's life. The close proximity of the Ascendant to the Moon suggests that John sided, at least on an intellectual level, with his mother; however, his heart may have remained on the side of his father.

Moon Ruler: ♄ ♏ in 9th

Saturn in Scorpio suggests a strongly judgmental or critical attitude, as well as a repression of the passions, particularly the sexual impulse. This restriction is felt most in the area of the need to extend experience to new horizons (9th).

Moon Aspects: ☽ □ ♄

Moon in square aspect with the Moon ruler reveals a powerful tension. A restrictive control over the modes of self-expression, and a constant awareness and judging of speech and writings. There is the possibility of a repressed mother complex, but the Moon also signifies the natural love interest in a man's chart. In John's case the attainment of his ideal mate—someone who is intelligent with a distant, dreaming manner and an air of mystery—is hindered by his excessive self-control and intellectualizing.

Mercury: ☿ ♐ in 10th

Mercury is in detriment in Sagittarius, and within a decan of Midheaven. This suggests an excess of thinking and brooding, and a nervous, excitable nature out of harmony with itself. Its presence in the 10th house indicates that the written or spoken communication of information or ideas plays an important part in John's life beyond the home and in the career. His is a restless mind constantly seeking after understanding and never fulfilled.

Mercury Aspects: ☿ ⚻ ♀

Mercury near Midheaven dominates Venus near Lower Midheaven and in conjunction with the South Node, through the aspect of minor tension called quincunx, even though Venus is inherently the more important factor (♀ ♂ rules). Mercury rules the 3rd house, which Venus occupies, stressing this dominance. An awkwardness and tension exists between the intellectual seeking and rationalizing, and the more visceral emotional urges of a close personal type.

Venus: ♀ ♉ in 3rd

Venus rules Taurus, and its action should be pure and powerful, but it is modified and subdued by its location near Lower Midheaven and its difficult aspects. Venus in Taurus shows a strongly affectionate nature, and the 3rd house suggests a need to be sociable and to express love in a casual, friendly manner toward family, neighbors, and other people who touch John's immediate personal environment. There is a strong need to fit in and to be liked by others.

Venus Aspects: ♀ ♂ ☋

Unfortunately the life principle of Venus is badly afflicted. Conjunction with the South Node means that John's naturally loving nature is being submerged or diminished—the South Node obscures or subdues by covering what it comes in contact with, whereas the North Node exalts and illuminates what it elevates within its jaws. Saturn is almost in conjunction with the North Node in Scorpio, suggesting that the principle of Saturn is exalted at the expense of Venus. An overly intellectual approach to life (♀ ♐ in 10th) and an excess of self-control with a sullen, censorious attitude (♄ ♏ in 9th) couple to suffocate a strong inherent tendency to give affection and an equally strong need to receive it.

Mars: ♂ ♊ in 4th

Suppressed sexuality resulting from difficulty and repression in the home environment as a child. Frustration produces quarrelsomeness, irritability, and an impulse to argue and be contrary that wastes energy. The sensual and lively part of John's personality is struggling to express itself but is inhibited. Mars in the first quine of Gemini almost seems to be yearning back toward Venus, striving to enter Taurus and unite with the planet of love. But they are held apart by double square aspects: ((♂ ♂ IC) □ A; (♀ ♂ ☋) □ ☉). Strong conflict lies between desire (♂) and its fulfillment (♀).

Mars Aspects: ♂ ♂ IC

Conjunction with Lower Midheaven shows that the impulses of masculine aggression and sexual potency have been pushed as deep into the darkness of the unconscious as they can possibly go.

♂ □ A

John is at war with his aggressive emotions. His anger is very tightly wound up and seldom exhibits itself—outwardly he appears calm and passive. However, the violent tension created by repressing aggression may let go at any time, resulting in a potentially dangerous explosion of rage.

Jupiter: ♃ ♍ in 7th

The desire for expression and growth will seek to realize itself in quiet, modest ways (♍). Partnerships, particularly the emotional and sexual bond of marriage, will be difficult to form—Jupiter is in detriment in Virgo. There is a tendency to adopt a cynical and arrogant air of superiority. Conscientiousness can be carried to extremes and result in needless worrying. John's attitude toward life is intellectual.

Jupiter Aspects: None

In some ways Jupiter is the most interesting planet in the chart because it stands alone and unaspected. There is a crying need to integrate this principle of John's life with the rest of the chart. Perhaps its isolation signifies that real personal growth cannot occur until the emotional need for love and society can be openly expressed and exist in harmony with the intellect, free at last of the crushing burden of self-judgment and criticism.

Saturn: ♄ ♏ in 9th

Saturn in Scorpio reveals a reserve and secrecy, a purposeful but brooding and selfish nature. This purposefulness is directed to a need to express and understand life in a region beyond the commonplace (9th). Very likely occult studies are being indicated. This interest amounts to a passion (♏). Not only is Saturn square with the Moon, it is very nearly in opposition to Venus, showing that John has difficulty in dealing with women, possibly the result of unresolved conflict with the mother or sister.

Nodes of the Moon: ☊ ♏ in 9th; ☋ ♉ in 3rd

The nodes always indicate a polarity of giving and taking. While something is lost or suppressed at the South Node, its energies are transferred to the head where something else is gained or exalted. In John's case the loss is love and affection that would ordinarily express itself through physical contact (♉) and social communication (3rd). The energies of these things are being redirected toward deep study and a search for the meaning of secret and hidden matters (9th), which is almost in the nature of an obsession (♏), so single-minded is it.

Node Aspects: (☊ ☋) □ ☉

The square aspects with the Sun emphasize the vital power of this polarity and the tension it is causing in John's life. He is literally being pulled apart by the conflict that results from his ignoring and suppressing the emotional bonds he badly needs in favor of an esoteric spiritual knowledge that ultimately will always lie just beyond his reach. The driving force of this polarity may be John's ambivalent love-hate relationship with his father.

6) *Rune Factors*

Ascendant: ᛩ ||

The overriding impulse is to transform (ᛩ) the aspects of the personality indicated by ♓ in the 1st house. John's persona is largely a frozen mask and a deception (|) that has become so firmly locked into place, it will be difficult to remove.

Midheaven: ᛏ ᚺ ᚺ

The ego, or essential and true self, suffers hardship and deprivation in its striving for expression and control.

Sun: ᚢ ᚠ ᚢ

The double appearance of Uruz (ᚢ) as qualifier of both the sign Leo and the Sun points to strong masculine potency and drive, which is reinforced by the fact that the Sun occupies its own sign. However, the presence of the quine rune Uruz under the influence of the quindecan rune Fehu (ᚠ) shows that this power does not act freely but is dependent or subservient to other factors in John's life.

Moon: ᚱ ᛩ ᛈ

Raido (ᚱ) is a striving after attainment, a seeking and a quest, in this case in pursuit (ᛩ) of some service to humanity (♒ in 12th). Perth (ᛈ) as the quine rune suggests that the driving force behind the seeking is a need for fulfillment and fullness on an emotional-sensory level.

Mercury: ᛏ ᚺ ᛏ

The life-principle of Mercury is influenced by a sense of duty, honor and a reverence for truth (ᛏ). Its expression will be hindered (ᚺ) and entail hardship (ᛏ) that will be protracted and mental rather than acute and physical.

Venus: X X Y

Sacrifice (X) of affection (♉) and loving relationships with friends and family (3rd) due to a conviction that love (♀) is somehow forbidden or taboo (Y).

Mars: ∫ ∫ ∫

Energetic action and sexual potency are subordinated or suppressed by a sense of duty. Eihwaz for ♊ in the 4th house suggests that the suppression arises from the family situation.

Jupiter: ˢ ˢ P

The Sowelu (ˢ) rune is the solar rune of destiny and retribution, the intervention of the hand of God in human affairs. The modesty and solitude of John's life is his inescapable karma, the result of his nature and environment. It must be lived; it cannot be denied. But the Wunjo (P) is spiritual rebirth and glory that stems from sacrifice and trials weathered. The experience gained through suffering will help in the growth of John's soul.

Saturn: Þ F ◊

Change (◊) resulting from knowledge (F) won as a result of suffering and personal torment (Þ). This change is of a restricting and limiting type (♄).

North Node: F Þ F

Difficulty in the communication of feelings leads to a conscious study of those feelings.

South Node: P X P

Loss and sacrifice of affections and feelings of love for a higher purpose of spiritual growth, which may not be willed or recognized on the conscious level.

7) Rune Card Spread

The central influence and the heart of the matter is Uruz (∩), masculine force, a testing and proving of masculinity in the passage from childhood to adulthood.

The row of the past reads change and transformation (◊) through a journey (R), the object of change being the transcendence of suffering of a hidden mental kind that is being endured (↑).

The row of the present reads sacrifice (X) of masculine pride (∩) out of a sense of duty or filial responsibility (∫).

The row of the future reads testing of the will by a burning away of the dross of materialism and selfish interests (ζ) through the suffering and enduring of humiliation, mockery, and scorn ($\flat$) in the difficult pursuit of wisdom ($\digamma$).

The left-hand column of the subject performing the action reads, from bottom to top, change or the turbulent need for change ($\diamond$), sacrifice (X) and the burning or cleansing power of the spirit (ζ).

The right-hand column of the object upon which this subject acts reads hardship and suffering ($\dagger$), duty and endurance ($\int$), in pursuit of truth ($\digamma$).

The central column of action reads a quest (R) requiring valor ($\sqcap$) in the face of scorn and torment from others ($\flat$).

The diagonal of obstruction, running from upper-right to lower-left on the card layout, reads divine retribution or karma (ζ) testing masculine potency and courage ($\sqcap$) with suffering ($\dagger$).

The diagonal of construction, running from lower-left to upper-right on the card grid, reads change ($\diamond$) through valor ($\sqcap$) in the pursuit of wisdom ($\digamma$).

8) Categories

Character

The overall character is emotional, creative, intellectual, and detached in its expression. A love of privacy and solitude reveals itself in the impulse to withdraw from the company of others.

There is a powerful vitality and force of will ($\odot$ Ω) that is shackled by an intense inner conflict, creating imbalance as parts of the nature are suppressed and distorted. The character is split down the middle between the essential need to be emotional, loving, and tactile, and the imposed need to be intellectual, controlled, and disciplined.

Personality

John is highly responsive to the attitudes and treatment of others, by turns elated or depressed as he is loved or rejected. He is impressionable and withdraws not because he dislikes society, but to protect his exposed and vulnerable feelings. The fear of rejection limits the degree to which he can express his loving and caring personality. He is self-critical and strains after an impossible ideal of perfection.

Identity

John is inclined to social communication, the free exchange of ideas and opinions, and likes to share himself with others. He has a natural skill in conveying difficult concepts and finding the right words. Modest about his attainments, he is shy with women and slightly awkward, and prefers to talk rather than to act, being at heart a romantic visionary.

Spiritual Level

There is a natural talent for mediumship ($\math;$ in 12th) and a strong interest in spiritual matters (A $\mathcal{H}$), which is not credulous, but highly analytical and critical ($\hbar$ in 9th; $\hbar \square \math;$). The driving force in John is a search after meaning (MC $\nearrow$ in 10th).

Mental Level

Skill exists for communicating on a personal level with others ($\varphi\; \bigtriangledown$ in 3rd) but it is suppressed ($\varphi\; \sigma\; \mho$) in favor of more abstract and profound studies ($\Omega\; \mathrm{M}$ in 9th). There is a deep interest in less conventional arts and sciences, the paranormal and the occult ($\varphi\; \nearrow$). Teiwaz ($\uparrow$) ruling in the quine of Mercury indicates that this fascination is driven by a love of truth.

Emotional Level

Tension dominates the emotions. The natural tenderness and affection is suppressed by an excess of intellectual analysis and criticism, both of self and others. The aggressive impulses are buried ($\sigma\; \sigma\; \mathrm{IC}$) causing an outward timidness, but they threaten to erupt (A $\square\; \sigma$) at any slight provocation. The openness and expansiveness of John's nature are cut off from the rest of his emotions, and the integration of this part of his character is badly needed to restore an emotional balance.

Physical Level

Sun in Leo, particularly because it is located twice by the Uruz ($\bigcap$) rune, indicates robust health and physical strength, along with great virility, even though the expression of this sexual potency is suppressed ($\sigma\; \sigma\; \mathrm{IC}$). Possible mental imbalance (($\math;$ 12th) $\square\; \hbar$) may ultimately cause a breakdown due to stress. Whether this is overt and results in hospitalization, or is concealed from others, it will have a limiting or confining effect. The reservoir of life force that John is able to draw upon may enable him to hide even a very serious mental problem for a prolonged period without detection.

Family

By John's own statement the home environment was strained. Tension existed with siblings (♀ ♂ ☊ in 3rd) and there was also anger and concealed frustration toward the parents (♂ ♂ IC in 4th). John felt he was being shunned or overlooked, probably by a sister (♈ over ♀) and may have felt that he was letting down one or both of his parents, probably his father, by not being as bold or outwardly masculine as he was expected to be (♌ over ♂). There was trouble between his parents resulting in a rupture between them, either a physical separation or an emotional separation. Outwardly John sided with his mother (A is near ☽); inwardly he was torn between them.

Friends

Friendships will be difficult to establish (11th is void). There will be an awkwardness in making warm, personal ties with acquaintances (♀ ♂ ☊ in 3rd) and a hesitation in reaching out beyond the immediate personal environment (♂ ♂ IC in 4th). In spite of the fact that John has an inherent skill in communicating (☿ in 10th), it does not extend to personal feelings (☿ ⚻ ♀).

Love

The house of sexual love (8th) and the house of love affairs and children (5th) are both void. John will probably be attracted to a woman who is intellectual and unconventional in her thinking, a visionary, but outwardly modest and quiet (☽ ♒ in 12th). His own behavior toward her is likely to be conscientious and reserved (♃ ♍ in 7th), and he must guard against an overly critical attitude (☽ □ ♄). It may be that the energies that would ordinarily go into marriage will be diverted to other commitments of an intellectual or spiritual nature.

Business

Teaching or writing are obvious career options (☿ in 10th). There may be a shyness that limits the ability to express ideas verbally (♃ ♍ ; (♀ ☊) ⚻ ☿) or convey them with the body through acting or dance (♂ ♂ IC), which is a pity since such expressions would probably be effective. John's real talent is for capturing and ordering nebulous impressions and vague intuitions into a coherent artistic creation, and presenting mystical or occult truths in a clear, practical manner.

He may be attracted to the ascetic or monastic life due to his interest in spiritual matters and the suppression of physical and emotional urges. This asceticism is likely to be philosophical rather than religious. He has an unlimited capacity for hard work ($\odot$ Ω in 6th) but should approach his metaphysical studies with caution ($\hbar$ in 9th) to prevent mental strain ($\hbar$ $\square$ $\mathbb{D}$). Money is unimportant to him (2nd and 8th, both void), therefore he is unlikely ever to become rich.

John's best chance for success lies in forming a partnership ($\mathbb{4}$ in 7th) that will supplement his weak character zones, ideally a marriage partnership.

Recreation

His innate pleasure in team sports will be limited by his difficulty in establishing personal rapport with others, while more independent pursuits such as skiing, mountain climbing and skydiving will appear too risky (σ σ LM; σ $\square$ A). Therefore interest is likely to channel into mental sports such as chess, or sports where little interaction with others, but fine judgment and skill, is required, such as archery and target shooting. Invention and design, games and puzzles, and spectator activities will attract. Gambling will appear too much of a foolish risk to be enjoyed.

Travel

Short trips revolve more around business than personal interests. Long trips and vacations are intended for intellectual growth and education, with pleasure a secondary motive. There is a strong need to see beyond the horizon and explore the distant vista (φ $\nearrow$; $\mathbb{4}$ $\mathbb{m}$), but because of the lack of physical boldness and the intellectual approach, this is likely to take the form of excursions in the imagination through escapist literature and mystical experiences. There is a danger of attraction to drugs and alcohol as instruments of escape, but the strong rational and critical factors may result in the analysis and rejection of these vehicles as dangerous and ultimately unproductive.

Runic Astrology Oracle

John Doe—Life Reading

Preface

Rune astrology is not an analysis of the positions of the planets in the heavens and should not be confused with horary astrology, which is the casting of a horoscope at the time a question is asked for the purpose of resolving that question. It is rather a form of divination that draws meaning from the symbolic components of astrology as they are patterned by the selection of a set of related runes. Each working of the oracle will yield a unique arrangement of symbols. No two charts will be the same. Yet each chart is drawn by the hand of Fate to reveal significant information that can be used to understand the past and plan for the future. Oracles are only as good as those who interpret them. Since no human being is perfect, all divination contains errors and should be treated as a suggestive guide rather than an infallible prophecy.

You are a man of strong emotions and deep convictions, with intuitive and creative skills. Sensitive to criticism and the slights of others, you are easily hurt but feel that you must hide your reactions. Rather than retaliate against injury, you withdraw from situations of conflict. This often results in unresolved frustration and inner tension. The same impulse sends you seeking escape from the harsh realities of life into a world of imagination and dreams. This is encouraged by a natural mediumistic gift and a need to see beyond the confines of your own limited reality.

There is considerable emotional tension that probably has its roots both in your own nature and in the home environment of your childhood, which was divisive and unhappy. Your father's alcoholism resulted in a rift between your parents that forced you to take sides. Although intellectually you place the blame for this conflict upon your father, unconsciously you wonder if you yourself are not at least in part responsible due to your failure to live up to your father's expectations. While siding with your mother, you wonder if she is also in part responsible for your father's condition. This produces a state of attraction-repulsion toward both parents.

Although you were born with a strong and energetic body and a determined will, you have a timidity by nature that results from your sensitivity and intellectualism coupled with an active imagination. This is a source of conflict, because you find that you cannot always be as bold or aggressive as you are prompted to be at first impulse. After the initial rush forward you think about what you are doing and draw back. This has hindered your ability to make friends and express yourself emotionally with the opposite sex, despite your inherent potent sex drive and need for social companionship.

The frustration of your yearning for love and friendship has driven your life energies into intellectual channels, where you find that you can function not only as well as others, but considerably better. Your mind is too far-seeking and imaginative for the discipline of science, which fails to satisfy your thirst for meaning. More than anything else you wish to make sense of the world and find your place in it. This explains your interest in Eastern philosophy and mysticism, both of which apply the highest intimations of being in a practical way to individual human living.

A career teaching such subjects as theology, philosophy, anthropology, archaeology, comparative religion, psychology, literary criticism, art appreciation, or any subject where imagination is coupled with profound thought and refined judgment and criticism will have a good chance of success. This is more likely to prosper through the medium of writing rather than classroom lecturing due to your awkwardness in relating to others. You will also do well in fiction writing and creative design, but will always be more comfortable behind the scenes than when you are center stage.

Consider the possibility of forming a partnership. In your fiction writing, collaboration with another writer will help to round out your work. An outgoing literary agent would be a great asset in presenting your work to publishers since you possess little skill in promoting yourself, because you tend to be self-critical, and also because your reverence for the truth makes it difficult for you to misrepresent your abilities. If you get into design work, try to find someone else to present your ideas. You need a promoter and "front man" to make the greatest use of your creative and critical talents.

The suppression of your strong sexual drive and the bottling up of your aggression may result in a dangerous explosion unless you are able to find activities such as meditation, exercise, and challenging sports to blow off steam. If this tension is not vented in controlled ways, you run the danger of becoming a walking volcano ready to erupt at every minor provocation. Once control is lost it will be difficult to regain.

Even if there is no physical outburst, your frustrated desire for love and affection coupled with your inability to freely express your feelings may cause a nervous breakdown or other mental problem. You will be inclined to conceal this condition, fearing a negative reaction from others, but should seek help by talking about your feelings and reaching out to others no matter how difficult this seems at the time. Because you are unusually strong and possess great endurance, you can continue to function under pressures that would incapacitate most people, but even you have a breaking point, and when you lose the rigid structure of your life it is apt to shatter into a thousand pieces.

The best chance you have to balance your nature is to form a close personal partnership with a woman who compliments your abilities and can lend emotional support in those areas where you feel less able to cope. This will be someone who is intelligent and witty, of a highly unconventional nature but modest in her outward manner and reserved, who like you has depths of feeling and qualities that are not obvious on the surface. Ideally she will possess good social skills to make up for those you lack, and will be a nurturing earth-mother type who will be able, and willing, to lend validity to your feelings when you doubt yourself.

If you are fortunate enough to meet such a woman, guard against your natural tendency to criticize and find fault. You must make a special effort to convey your feelings of love to her—otherwise she may miss them, so deeply buried are they beneath your social reserve. You tend to be utterly devoted to those who reach out to you with friendship or love, but they may not realize your feelings because you are so skillful at hiding them.

It will never be easy for you to make friends. You must put extra energy into the process to overcome your inertia and literally break the ice that imprisons your emotions. Guard against an outwardly critical and judgmental air, which may be interpreted as a feeling of superiority. Also beware of giving in to frustration, which will make you appear sullen and depressing in the eyes of others.

Do not take so much to heart the things others say and do. Instead of working so hard to present a mask of outward indifference, try to find an inner balance and tranquility that will not flinch and tremble at every harsh word. Remember that you alone create the social climate around you, and you alone are responsible for the way others perceive and treat you. Since your power over these things is absolute, you have the potential to change them for the better.

Signs of a spiritual quest run through your life chart. Ultimately this may be what your existence on earth is all about. Although it seems to you that your weakness in social and personal relations is beyond your control, this is really not the case. It is beyond your immediate conscious control, but your higher mind is causing this personal weakness for a purpose. Perhaps it is necessary for you to channel and redirect your emotional energies into a search for meaning. The attainment of a spiritual understanding of your life may be what your life is focused upon, the lower needs and emotions being sacrificed for the higher.

This is not necessarily an evil state of affairs, even though it seems hard to you today. You may be sacrificing present pleasure and well-being for the future growth of your soul. The question you must seriously examine is whether or not your present suffering is really necessary, or are you inflicting it upon yourself to no purpose? Ultimately you are the only one who can answer this question.

The kind of pervasive tension that exists in your chart always shows hardship and unhappiness. However, with dynamic tension there is the potential for change and growth. Those who have only harmonious aspects in their charts are destined to live comfortable, pleasant, and trivial lives. Such charts lack the energy that drives transformation and allows great things to occur. Your chart has this potential for greatness. But with it is an equal potential for disaster. You must come to terms with the conflicts in your life so that they do not tear you apart. If you are able to do this, your life may produce some work of enduring importance.

In the end, your only enemy is yourself. Guard against self-pity and despair. Take care that you do not begin to hate your own life. Fight against the impulse to pull away from pain—this is a futile reflex since there will come a time when you cannot retreat any farther. Resist bitterness and cynicism. Above all, beware of seeking escape in drugs or alcohol. It will do no good for you to repeat the errors of your father. Persist in efforts to reach out to others even when these appear foredoomed to failure, and remember that your life has a purpose that it is your duty to seek and fulfill.

16

Sample Career Reading

The second sample reading is concerned with the career situation and outlook of a working mother who wished to discover what the most promising options were for her professional future. Although the subject of this second reading is narrower than the first, for the sake of completeness, all the categories have been considered in order to demonstrate how they can be weighted toward a single question. In practice, some categories might be omitted at the discretion of the diviner when the reading takes a very specific focus.

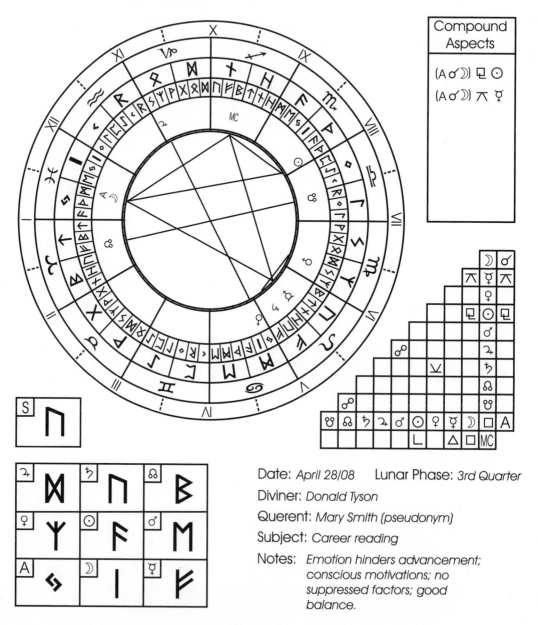

Compound Aspects

Date: *April 28/08*   Lunar Phase: *3rd Quarter*

Diviner: *Donald Tyson*

Querent: *Mary Smith (pseudonym)*

Subject: *Career reading*

Notes: *Emotion hinders advancement; conscious motivations; no suppressed factors; good balance.*

Figure 16-1

Reading Two

Querent: Mary Smith (pseudonym)

Subject: Career reading

Mary is a working mother in her early thirties. She has two small children. Her husband is employed as a government office clerk. Mary manages a busy bowling center in a downtown shopping mall. This places her on call into the small hours of the morning seven days a week. She complains of friction with her employers, who refuse to hire an assistant manager to take some of the burden off her shoulders. Whenever there is a problem, she is called in from her home to deal with it. The owners of the bowling alley are slow to put up the money even for basic day-to-day operating expenses. Seeking a raise is a process of protracted guerrilla warfare. Mary feels she is being underpaid and overworked, yet is reluctant to abandon a much needed second paycheck. She would like to establish a new career as a travel tour operator but is hesitant about leaving the familiarity and relative security of her present job to take on a risky new business venture that would often separate her from her husband and children.

1) Significator Rune: Uruz (ᚢ)

This is the rune of courage and testing of mettle, of forcefulness and free will, of passage by trial into a new phase of life. The trial may be hard and perhaps an extended effort.

2) Overall Pattern: Splay

Four planets are grouped in and around Leo, with the Moon in conjunction with the Ascendant in Pisces, not far removed from the North Node in Aries. Interests are widely distributed with a focus of attention on balancing the performance of duty (♍ and 6th) and the fulfillment of self (5th) while maintaining authority (♃ ♌) at work and in the home (♂ ♋ in 5th). The three aspects radiating from Midheaven and the fact that the quarter of the chart around Lower Midheaven is empty indicate a healthy openness and conscious purpose.

3) Astrological Groups

Compound aspects—(A♂☽) ⊑ ☉ ; (A ♂ ☽) ⊼ ☿

Conjunctions—A ♂ ☽

Outstanding planets—♄ ♌ (detriment); ♀ ♍ (fall) ; ♂ ♋ (fall); ♃ ♑ (fall)

Polarity—Positive: 3 (MC ☿ ♄); Negative: 6 (A ☽ ♃ ☉ ♀ ♂)

Qualities—Cardinal: 2 (♃ ♂)
Fixed: 3 (☉ ☿ ♄)
Mutable: 4 (A MC ☽ ♀)

Elements—Fire: 3 (MC ☿ ♄)
Water: 4 (A ♂ ☽ ☉)
Air: 0
Earth: 2 (♃ ♀)

4) Rune Groups

Families—Fehu: 3 (ᚠ ᚨ ᛜ)
Hagalaz: 3 (ᚼ ᛁ ᛏ)
Teiwaz: 3 (ᛘ ᛉ ᛒ)

Elements—Fire: 3 (ᚠ ᛜ ᛒ)
Water: 4 (ᚼ ᛁ ᚱ ᛘ)
Air: 0
Earth: 2 (ᛏ ᛗ)

5) Astrological Factors

Ascendant: ♓

In relation to career, Pisces indicates a general nature that is easygoing and sensitive, un-worldly and impressionable, submissive, readily moved to tears, tending to withdraw from the harsh realities where possible. Mary is receptive to ideas, with a creative imagination, but she can become overemotional and be too soft. Her faults are touchiness, indecisive-ness, and a desire to believe others that allows her to be easily taken in. She can be extrava-gant and temperamental at times.

Ascendant Ruler: ♃ ♑ in 11th

A resourcefulness and sense of responsibility in meeting production goals allows oppor-tunities for expansion to be seized and exploited (♃ ♑). There is a conscientiousness to achieve work goals for the benefit of others (♃ in 11th) with a lesser regard for self.

Ascendant Aspects: A ♂ ☽

Mary responds in an instinctive, emotional way without thinking things through. She falls easily into work habits and routines, and is reluctant to break with the past. Changeable and restless, needing to be always on the move, she sometimes has feelings of discontent. There is a strong dependence on the mother.

A ⊡ ☉

Her protective, responsible attitude toward work results in a minor clash of wills with a male, perhaps exacerbated by sexual attitudes and the desire of the male to dominate the situation. Mary is reluctant to share resources or authority (☉ in 8th) due to her excessive sense of personal responsibility.

A ⊼ ☿

The conscious need to exert authority over the business (☿ ♌) in order to maintain efficiency and financial health and fulfill her responsibilities (☿ in 6th) results in worry, nervousness and a concern about losing control. There is a conflict between the basic nature (A ♂ ☽ in ♓), which is submissive and easily dependant, and the need to dominate the work situation and give orders (☿ ♌), which is causing mental and nervous stress.

Sun: ☉ ♏ in 8th

A self-sacrifice of inner harmony and the sense of wholeness in order to share resources and possessions with others who are dependant. Determined endurance with no complaint uttered, even though at times the feeling is one of being torn apart by conflicting needs.

Sun Ruler: ♂ ♋ in 5th

Activities (♂) in the field of management (5th) will be conservative and defensive, designed to protect what has been attained (♋).

Sun Aspects: ☉ ⊡ ☽

A minor disharmony or division in the life that is the result of a need to accomplish goals connected with the expression of the personality and separate interests of the self (1st), and goals that are connected with the material and emotional dependence of others (8th). The roots of this conflict may lie in the relations Mary had with her parents during her childhood.

☉ ∟ MC

There is a tendency to be a bit overbearing in an effort to ensure that work and rewards are shared equitably, and a feeling on Mary's part that she knows best what people should be doing to get the most from their efforts. This can result in personality clashes and ego conflicts.

Moon: ☽ ♓ in 1st

Mary's manner of dealing with the public is sympathetic and receptive (☽ ♓). She reacts strongly to the words and actions of others, leading to many ups and downs in her professional relationships (☽ in 1st). The working atmosphere around her can change rapidly and produce an emotional rollercoaster ride.

Moon Ruler: ♃ ♑ in 11th

Jupiter is in fall in Capricorn, suggesting a tendency to adopt a self-righteous attitude in public dealings. Too great a sense of responsibility results in austerity or meanness in allocating resources, and this leads to resentment on the part of others, who then suddenly turn against Mary, seemingly without cause.

Moon Aspects: ☽ ⚻ ☿

Indecision leads to worry and nervous strain. Often a business decision is made abruptly and without sufficient consideration, just to get the problem over with so that it will not weigh upon the mind. Worrying about too many small details all at once causes forgetfulness. There is an underlying desire to forget all worries so that they can no longer be a burden.

Mercury: ☿ ♌ in 6th

An innate talent for public communication that is optimistic and discerning. Mary has a gift for analyzing others and making them feel good, but sometimes her own sensitivity causes her to become rude or dejected in her expressions, or to adopt a hypercritical or prejudiced attitude that works against her own best interests.

Venus: ♀ ♍ in 6th

Modesty and shyness result in coolness and reserve in the expression of private feelings—Venus is in fall in Virgo. The work environment must be clean and orderly. Poor sanitation, especially around food, will not be tolerated, and vulgarity or coarseness of behavior causes inner distress and unhappiness. Mary is always ready to help others if it will make things run more smoothly, and spends a lot of time fussing over details to create harmony between her employees.

Venus Aspects: ♀ ⊥ ♄

The need is felt to control and limit the expression of affection toward others in order to maintain discipline. Much support is demanded of close friends and family, and if this is not forthcoming, disappointment and loneliness result. Always there is conscious awareness of the balance that must be achieved on the job between outgoing warmth and emotional restraint.

Mars: ♂ ♋ in 5th

Passionate possessiveness (♂ ♋) toward the family and the home, with strong protective and nurturing feelings toward her children (5th), who are a primary source of happiness. Managing and caring for the home is very fulfilling, while directing the education of her children serves as a creative extension of the self that is both challenging and rewarding.

Mars Aspects: ♂ ☍ ♃

A fundamental opposition of needs exists between the furtherance of the career (♃ ♑) and the passionate protectiveness toward the home (♂ ♋). Concern for the family is inhibiting growth of the career. At the same time career concerns are conflicting with family relationships. These poles pull upon the essential self with roughly equal force.

Jupiter: ♃ ♑ in 11th

Practicality and a willingness to work hard (♑) present opportunities in the area of organizing group activities (11th) that can result in an expansion of the scope of the career (♃ ♑). Mary has a gift for leading social functions, organizing and promoting group excursions, hosting parties and other collective gatherings, but this activity clashes with her devotion and protectiveness toward her own family (♃ ♑ ☍ ♂ ♋). Jupiter is in fall in Capricorn.

Saturn: ♄ ♌ in 5th

The need to exert authority and appear self-assured in the workplace is often frustrating and painful. Mary does not feel as confident as she must pretend to be in order to maintain control. She wishes she were more commanding and impressive in the eyes of others and finds the effort to pretend emotionally limiting.

Nodes of the Moon: ☊ ♈ in 1st; ☋ ♎ in 7th

A focus of attention and a giving of conscious life energies to the leadership role that projects the querent actively into the greater community (☊ ♈ in 1st). A subordination and a drawing upon the unconscious energies that go into identifying with an individual or individuals on a close personal level (☋ ♎ in 7th). Mary is metaphorically "sitting" upon her intimate relationships with her family and friends in order to elevate her impersonal professional objectives, which she regards as challenging and exciting.

6) Rune Factors
Ascendant: ᛟ   ᛟ   ᛗ

Much activity (ᛟ) of a self-centered, personal nature directed to the expression of individual needs and interests (1st) that is dependent upon and productive of great intellectual or mental exertion and worry.

Midheaven: ᚺ   ᚺ   ↑

Disruption and confusion (ᚺ) connected with long travel and attempts to extend the personal horizon (♐ in 9th). This travel is looked upon as bold and exciting, but may lead to strife (↑).

Sun: ᚠ   ᚦ   ᚦ

This may be a masculine influence (☉) at work seeking to control or dominate (♏) by spreading malicious lies (ᚦ) or speaking against the querent (ᚠ). This malice is designed to cast Mary out of the center and destroy her integration with her environment—possibly to have her removed from her job. Alternately, these runes could be read as conflict over work with her husband.

Moon: ᛁ   ᛟ   ᛗ

Emotional and intellectual turmoil is concealed beneath a placid, attractive surface. Stress is hidden from others.

Mercury: ᚠ   ᚾ   ᛏ

The job is a kind of enslavement to the pursuit of wealth (ᚠ), but Mary persists doggedly in an effort to prove herself in the eyes of others (ᚾ), resulting in mental suffering (ᛏ over ☿).

Venus: ᛏ ᛏ ᛋ

This appears to be a warning (ᛏ)—cease denying personal feelings or lightning will strike (ᛋ) in the form of some emotional crisis.

Mars: ᛗ ᛗ ᛈ

There is control over the events at home. The querent applies good judgment (ᛗ) to situations and problems (ᛗ) to get her own way (ᛈ), and she is usually right in her choices.

Jupiter: ᛟ ᚷ ᛋ

The expansive power of Jupiter carries a price tag (ᛋ) that has to do with the home (ᚷ), and the silver lining of success is limited in duration (ᛟ). For everything gained there is a cost.

Saturn: ᚢ ᚠ ᚢ

The giving of orders that restrict the actions of others and place limits upon spending and waste is outwardly bold and forceful, but inwardly a conflict exists, and Mary has the feeling of being used for the gain of others rather than acting in her own best interests. She is forced to play the part of the bully and the spoilsport because of unseen constraints placed upon her by her superiors, but she receives most of the blame.

North Node: ᛒ ↑ ᚠ

Love and affection (ᛒ) is set at strife (↑) with the need to attain financial security (ᚠ).

South Node: ᛜ ᛁ ᚱ

The dream (ᛁ) of a balanced and harmonious home life (ᛜ) is still some distance away and must be pursued (ᚱ). This is where the secret heart lies—with family and hearth. The querent's life quest, of which she is not conscious, is to create an ideal, perfect home environment with herself at its center.

7) Rune Card Spread

The central influence is Ansuz (ᚠ), which means communication or eloquent persuasion.

The row of the past reads cyclical activity (ᛈ) with periods of inaction (ᛁ) for the purpose of material gain (ᚠ)—a basic description of the bowling business with its highs and lows tied to seasonal changes. It might also signify inner turmoil beneath a pleasant mask of exterior calm in pursuit of money.

The row of the present reads an emotional distancing or warding off (Υ) as a defense mechanism, and the skillful and perhaps insincere use of words (ᚠ) as a means to an end (M).

The row of the future shows cyclical satisfaction (ᚹ) as the result of an excess of willfulness and force (ᚢ) in seeking the ultimate objective, love and pleasure (ᛒ).

The column of the subject on the left of the card spread reads change or turbulence (ᛊ), a defensive posture (Υ) resulting in a period of perceived success (ᚹ).

The column of the object on the right of the spread, to which the subject refers, reads material possessions or wealth (ᚠ) but also servitude as a vehicle of attainment (M) of the ultimate goal, love and well-being (ᛒ).

The column of action, in the middle of the card spread, reads an unwelcome and troubling lack of progress (ᛁ) caused by a subtle persuasion (ᚠ) based upon a willfulness or stubbornness—perhaps a need by the one causing the delay to exercise a masculine dominance (ᚢ).

The diagonal of obstruction, traversing the spread from upper-left to lower-right, reads clarity of purpose (ᚹ) eloquently expressed (ᚠ) motivated by greed or the desire to possess (ᚠ). The diagonal of construction, extending from the lower-left to the upper-right, reads a turning on its head (ᛊ) of the obstructive argument (ᚠ) in order to attain pleasure and fulfillment (ᛒ).

8) Categories

Character

Sensitive, outgoing, optimistic, with emotions that lie very close to the surface. A bright, creative imagination that is open to new ideas and experiences. The overall pattern is one of balance between duty to others (☉ ♏ in 8th) and personal aspirations (A ♂ ☽ ♓ in 1st). Mary is conscientious about meeting her obligations because she does not wish to disappoint those who rely on her. She takes things too much to heart and is easily hurt, but does not often reveal her pain, choosing rather to submerge it beneath the surface.

Personality

The mask presented to the world is professionally cheerful and expansive (♃ ♑ in 11th), if somewhat artificial and cool at times. Emotions play a strong part in determining persona (A ♂ ☽), which will be quite variable (♓) and at the same time adaptive as it is influenced by underlying vitality and personal needs (☉) and the shaping power of critical intellect (☿), both of which bear upon the public mask in stressful but energizing ways.

Identity

In a professional sense the true aspirations of the querent, the way she sees herself ideally, are being retarded and restrained in their unfolding by a male influence (♂ in 5th) which is preventing her from becoming all that she might otherwise become (♂ ☍ ♃ ♑). This influence derives its power over Mary from her concern for the home environment (♂ ♋). Nonetheless she is doing a good job of balancing her professional, public aspirations (☊ in 1st) with her personal, private relationships (☋ in 7th).

Spiritual Level

There is an inherent sensitivity to hidden occult currents (☉ in 8th) and an urge to bring them into the light and explain them (MC in 10th) that might easily express itself in superstitious beliefs due to the impressionable, passive mind of the querent. A desire to know a higher reality (MC ♐) will likely confine itself to conventional sources such as the established church (☿ in 6th).

Mental Level

Excellent skills exist to structure and define objectives creatively within a limited budget (♄ in 5th). There is talent for public speaking (☿ in 6th). Mary is a good organizer and leader of community social events. She has a capacity to learn, particularly in areas that express her function in the community (MC in 10th).

Emotional Level

Emotions are deep and strong (A ☽ ☉ ♂ in water signs; MC in fire sign), but somewhat suppressed (♀ ♍ in 6th; ♀ ⊼ ♄). There is natural skill in socializing (♃ in 11th) and forming public acquaintances, and this is very useful in a business that entails frequent public contact. Emotional responses are automatic and can easily fly out of control, requiring a constant awareness of this danger (☿ ⊼ ☽).

Physical Level

Physical health is good, but there is the possibility of illness in sexual organs (☉ ♏ in 8th) such as the breasts, womb, etc. that may require an operation (♂ ♋), as well as a susceptibility to allergies, sinus problems, ear infections, and throat infections (☉ ♏ reflex to ♉). There is also potential injury to the back in a fall (♄ ♌ in 5th). Care should be taken that business worries do not lead to chronic stomach upset or ulcers (♃ ♑ reflex ♋; ♃ ☍ ♂).

Family

Concern is focused upon the husband and children. There is worry that the children will grow up out of control due to the time away from them on business, and perhaps an over-compensation and the attempt to impose an excess of discipline during the time spent at home (♄ ♌ in 5th). There is concern that the husband (♂ ♋ in 5th) is unhappy over these business demands, and also that Mary's mother, who provides daycare for the children, is replacing her in their affections ((A ☌ ☽) ⚻ ☿ 5th).

Friends

Mary has good skill in arbitrating personal disputes and restoring harmony, along with a desire to fit into the social pattern and thereby be at oneness with the group (☿ ♌ in 6th). To some extent, these tendencies are limited by emotion and the temptation to take sides in arguments (☽ ⚻ ☿). The ability to establish new friendships (♃ in 11th) is hindered by a shyness or reluctance to reach out beyond the home and the personal sphere (♃ ☍ ♂ ♋ in 5th). Power to attract new friends (♀) is limited by enforced control over the emotions (♀ ⚺ ♄).

Love

There is a strong sexual energy (☉ ♏ in 8th), which is highly possessive (♂ ♋) and potentially jealous. This energy is focused upon the home (♂ in 5th). To some extent the marriage is being slighted or sacrificed (☋ in 7th) in favor of Mary's self-centered interests (☊ in 1st), but there is great resentment when the shoe is on the other foot.

Business

Efforts to expand and develop the career (♃ ♑) are being willfully frustrated (♃ ☍ ♂) by another person. There is an intellectual and emotional capacity for work (☿ and ♀ in 6th), but new career horizons are limited (☋ in 7th). The money outlook (☉ in 8th), though potentially very positive, is hindered by the inability to refrain from emotional expressions (☽ □ ☉). A reluctance to take new initiatives is tied to concerns over the home situation (♂ ♋ in 5th).

Recreation

Recreation and business are wrapped up in each other; not surprising, since the business is a recreational activity. There is an interest in speculation and gambling ($\u263F$ $\u264C$) but this will be limited in its actual expression due to a self-imposed limit on risk-taking ($\u2644$ $\u264C$) and a sense of responsibility to the home that moderates the impulse to take a chance ($\u2642$ $\u264B$ in 5th). Social activities ($\u2643$ in 11th) and community service (MC in 10th) will be enjoyed.

Travel

The impulse to extend outward and take risks will find outlet in career advancement (MC $\u2650$ in 10th). There is a need to balance productive work interests ($\u260A$ $\u2648$ in 1st) with the maintenance of close interpersonal relationships ($\u260B$ $\u264E$ in 7th).

Runic Astrology Oracle

Mary Smith—Career Reading

Preface

(See previous example for preface.)

The emotions are dominant in your character, which is sensitive to the surrounding environment and responds quickly to the words and actions of others, both receptively by what you feel, and expressively by the way you project those feelings. You are conscious of this sensitivity and seek to keep it under intellectual control so that it will not carry you away and cause you to do or say something you would later regret.

Consciously your interests are self-centered, which is not the same as selfish. You are preoccupied with your own goals and achievements, and examine every situation first in terms of how it relates to you, and only later in the way it may affect others. This self-interest is the result of your strong feelings—feelings are necessarily very personal. You are not particularly good at dispassionate analysis. Even when you are not involved in a situation, you involve yourself emotionally and analyze it as it relates to your beliefs and purposes.

In business, particularly for those in a position of authority, too much emotion can be a liability. You must maintain a balancing act between a natural impulse to sympathize and the need to be critical and restrictive. This has produced a certain amount of personal tension in your life.

Tension also arises out of your sense of duty to those who have placed their trust in you. You feel obligation to do a good job for your employers, and also to do well as a wife and mother. On the other side of the scale is your aspiration to express your own needs and find pleasure and contentment. This shows itself in a longing for travel to distant places (travel is an escape from responsibility, especially when it can be rationalized as a necessary business trip, which reduces the guilt that might otherwise arise).

There is a male influence in your chart who hinders your career by speaking about you in a negative way in order to hold back your advancement. Tension also arises from the resulting inability to expand and grow. This male is motivated by a need to remain in control, probably due to his own insecurity.

Although you are naturally frugal with resources that have been entrusted to you, even you cannot work miracles. Resentment may arise in your employees because you withhold funds or supplies from them that they legitimately need. Try to make them understand you are doing the best with what has been allocated to you, and that you are not the villain. Though careful with the resources of others, you have a streak of extravagance in your own nature and should guard against costly impulse buying.

It is necessary to make compromises between career and family if both are to be maintained at the same time. Right now you are doing a good job at keeping a balance between the two, but there is a danger of neglecting the home environment for the work environment. Since your children are especially important to you, a conscious awareness of the need for attending to both areas of life is vital if this healthy situation is to continue.

There exists a potential for nervous disorders brought on by the continuing strain of juggling work and family concerns. This may also manifest itself in chronic infections of the ears, nose, and throat, or bleeding stomach ulcers. Back strain from overwork is also possible.

The job you hold is well suited to your economizing, responsible, and social nature. You are good at organizing group activities or excursions, can look after money, and are able to express your thoughts clearly. The danger is that you are too good at what you do, and may be tempted to take on more work than you can handle. Do not be afraid to delegate responsibility to others. Recognize that they will make mistakes and be willing to tolerate a certain number of them. Give yourself some free time to relax and spend with your family.

Also realize that you can only do so much with the resources that are given to you. If you fail, recognize that it is not your fault and let it go. Nothing is gained by worrying that you cannot accomplish something that is impossible in the first place. Your employers may tend to use your strong sense of personal responsibility to those working under you to squeeze out the last penny of value from their allocations of supplies, and in so doing, push you beyond the limit of your ability to cope. Guard against this abuse by seeking slightly larger allocations of funds and materials than you actually need in order to give yourself a cushion to fall back on.

Do not become frustrated if your suggestions are not followed and your innovations ignored. There is a negative attitude toward you in the higher ranks of your company that may evolve and improve over time. Your communication skills and sense of responsibility make you a valuable asset, and your employers know this even if they do not wish to admit it. One function of taking responsibility is that others come to rely on you. This places you in a position of some power if you wish to exercise it to your advantage. You probably have more bargaining room than you realize.

It is easy for you to form habits and fall into a routine that makes you feel you are becoming trapped or stifled. Do not be afraid to try an approach that is wildly different from time to time, just to bang the rust off your life and energize your creativity. For you the dull routine is natural even when it is not pleasant. Breaking loose can be more difficult, and you must make an extra effort periodically to avoid stagnation.

Be firm in seeking vacation time, during which you have absolutely no contact with your work, and spend it with your family. Since you love to travel and see distant places, you might plan a family trip for a week or two every summer that is purely for fun. This type of release is more necessary for you than it would be for most people because of the burden you take upon your shoulders.

At some time in the future, it might be useful to integrate your business skills with your family life by leaving your present job and taking on a small business of your own that your husband and children could help you manage. This will to some extent reduce the trade-off of your attention between your work and your home, and make your life more integrated.

There are no dark corners or suppressed drives in your life that threaten to emerge with destructive force. On the contrary, your subconscious is remarkably clear and tranquil. All the factors influencing your life are in plain sight or very close to the surface. Considering the trade-off you are making between work and home, your chart is well balanced. It can be said that you are doing the best that might reasonably be expected of you under the circumstances. Provided this balance is not upset by unreasonable expectations on your part that focus on one particular area of your life, the outlook for the future is positive.

Things to Consider

When the querent first enters the room where the reading is to occur, it is important to take careful note of his or her manner. This should be done in an intuitive rather than an intellectual way. It is amazing how much information can be gained in a single glance. Whether the person is calm or nervous, healthy or sickly, extroverted or introverted, bright or dull, agreeable or sullen, well-groomed or slovenly, clean or dirty, well dressed or poorly dressed, happy or sad—all these and countless other subtle messages are conveyed in a moment. They are not formally expressed in words within the conscious mind, but the unconscious has gathered them in and already has begun to formulate an automatic, visceral response to the other person.

You should not even attempt to express these impressions to yourself. This is the method of charlatans who often seek to make a lucky guess about their clients based upon their appearance and manner, or prior information gathered about them, in order to impress the querent with their occult power. Bringing initial impressions into the conscious mind actually inhibits the mediumistic faculty. They should be allowed to work in the depths of the unconscious during the reading, where they will automatically shape the interpretation of the chart.

Some astrologers regard astrology as a science, and disdain anything so fallibly human as intuition in reading the horoscope. This is an unfortunate view, because all divination is ultimately patterned by the intuitive power of the diviner. Intuition is the guide that limits the infinite complexity of any method of divination and directs it with a specific intent upon a single narrow but productive path to the solution of the question in the mind of the querent.

Ask the querent what he or she seeks to learn through the oracle. Receive the response passively and allow it to flow unmolested into the depths of your psyche. At the same time be aware of the way the response is phrased and the tone and quality of the querent's voice. All these bits of information are added in an organic manner to the process of divination.

In the ancient world, the sibyls of Greece and the augurs of Rome did not conceive themselves as the formulators of the response, but only as the mediums or conduits through which the response passed. It was the gods who gave answers—the diviners were only the instruments, the mouths through which higher spiritual intelligences spoke. It is still useful in modern divination to retain this sense of detachment from the response, to become like a sheet of clear glass that lets light pass unimpeded and untinted. An emotional reaction to the querent that is allowed to manifest itself, either as a feeling of attraction-repulsion, or an intellectualized "I like you—I don't like you," will severely limit the usefulness of the divination.

Today we would be more likely to regard the responses of the oracle as expressions of some part of our hidden being—our unconscious, our spirit, our higher self—rather than as the intervention of gods or spirits. But the principle of passivity still applies. Our higher mind cannot convey its answer to the querent's question through our conscious mind unless our conscious mind is calm and still. A lake passes on the image of a distant mountain when its waters are peaceful, but cannot transmit the impression of the mountain when it is stirred by the wind.

In consulting the runic astrology oracle for yourself or for others, it important to maintain a serious, professional attitude. Always treat the divination with respect, and hold in your mind the clear expectation that what you read from the chart will be important information that can be put to use in a practical way.

Your seriousness communicates itself to the querent, who then places greater value on the results of the reading. It also causes the querent to concentrate intensely on the subject of the divination during the actual casting of the chart. More than this, a serious, businesslike approach helps to focus your own attention and heightens the significance of your interpretation. The more you expect from the oracle, the more you will receive.

Whenever you cast a runic astrology chart for someone else, either as a friend or as a professional who is paid for the service, you will succeed or fail depending on how well you handle two distinct stages of the process.

The first stage is the actual erection of the chart, where you sit opposite the querent with the large chart between you both and go through the procedure of drawing the rune cards and placing the planet counters on the zodiac. It is possibly to consult the oracle using only the small chart, but if you do so, you lose the presentation value of the large chart, which is considerable. When you lay the counters one by one on the quines of the large chart, the querent is able to follow what you are doing and actually see how the chart is being built up step by step. To make this even clearer, you should explain in a simple way how the placement of the planets is established.

You will find that once the querent realizes what is going on, he or she will begin to anticipate by searching for the card rune around the quindecans of the zodiac, and then looking for the die upon the elemental triangle that corresponds in color to the color of the selected zodiac sign. This involvement has a positive effect on the divination. The energy of interest aroused in the querent communicates itself through the casting of the dice and helps to form a truly meaningful chart.

It is poor practice to enter the card runes and the positions of the planets on the small chart while you are in the process of laying the counters on the large chart. This breaks the concentration of querent and diviner alike. Always wait until all the rune cards have been turned and the entire large chart is laid out before recording the information on the small chart.

Once you have gained sufficient skill in interpreting the aspects and rune combinations, you will be able to carry on a reading while you are laying out the large chart. Naturally, your results will not be as detailed or as penetrating as they would if you spent several days making a comprehensive analysis of the chart, but they will still possess considerable value to the querent, and they will gain added interest from their organic relationship to the physical placing of the counters.

The large chart is especially effective in circumstances where you are expected to give a number of readings in a short span of time, for example at psychic fairs or social gatherings. Under these conditions the small chart may be dispensed with altogether. Even then, always treat the oracle with due respect. If the divinations threaten to turn into one big joke, terminate them at once.

In any kind of divination a certain amount of showmanship is necessary to heighten the awareness and maintain the interest of the querent. When you lay out the large chart, you are putting on a performance. The divination is a personal drama with symbolic archetypes for actors presented on the stage of the large chart. As diviner you are the narrator of this drama. It is your job to make sure the audience of one—the querent—understands what is taking place. If the querent does not understand, he or she will quickly lose interest and the dynamic energy of the presentation will fail. The actors—the runes—will have no source from which to take their meanings; their exposition of the play will begin to lose its force.

Never talk over the head of the querent or try to explain in a few minutes relationships it may have taken you weeks or months to understand; at the same time, do not ignore the querent's natural interest in the oracle and desire to follow what is happening from moment to moment. Gauge your exposition of the chart to the querent's level of comprehension. If you are reading for a child, keep your words simple and light. If reading for a person of business or a professional, be direct and specific when you explain what you are doing and where your interpretations arise.

The second stage at which you will either succeed or fail is the detailed written analysis you prepare for the querent as a permanent record of the divination. Since you have hours or days to consider what you will say in this report, it should be much more comprehensive than the intuitive, quick reading you take from the large chart as you lay it out. While you prepare the written report, the querent will wait in considerable anticipation for your results. The greater the anticipation, the greater the disappointment will be if your report is difficult to read, or hard to understand, or worst of all, contains nothing that the querent can apply in a practical, meaningful way in his or her life.

The querent is always looking to the diviner to provide something useful. This need not be in the form of actual advice; it may be an explanation of an existing situation that has puzzled the querent, or an avenue in life where the potential exists for growth, or the revelation of a stumbling block the querent has kept hidden in the unconscious and refused to face. But it must be something that can be acted upon. Vague, mystical generalizations will not satisfy the querent.

The written report will in large measure determine in the querent's mind your degree of professionalism. A sloppy, careless report written in ballpoint pen with mistakes crossed out cannot fail to make a bad impression, no matter how brilliant the actual analysis it conveys. It will also discourage anyone else who sees it from ever consulting you. Where possible, type your reports or have them typed. Thanks to the personal computer, this task is much less laborious than it used to be. The report can be entered into the computer file and a perfect copy for your client run off on the printer in one step.

For the same reasons, always mark the runes, aspect symbols and aspect lines, and glyphs of the planets on the small chart with great care. Aspect lines should be drawn with a straight edge. Use red ink for drawing the runes and to mark difficult aspects, and blue ink for the easy aspects. The aspect symbols can also be marked in red and blue if you wish. This results in an attractive and clear presentation that is both pleasant to look at and easy to read.

It is a simple matter to lay one small chart over another and join them at the top edge with a spring clip (a clipboard works quite well), then slip a sheet of carbon paper between them so that as you fill out the top chart for the querent, a second carbon reproduction is made for your own files. The carbon copy will not possess the red and blue colors, but these are mainly decorative and are not necessary in order to read the chart, or the small chart can be scanned and a duplicate printed.

It is a good idea to begin the written report with a brief preface similar to the one I have already given in the sample life reading of chapter sixteen. The preface distinguishes the runic astrology oracle from regular horary astrology to prevent confusion between the two, and states clearly that no divination of any kind is infallible. The querent should never be misled into believing that the advice of the diviner, no matter how well considered or learned it may be, has the authority of holy writ. The oracle may be perfect, but human beings make mistakes.

Every divination is ultimately about one person. Usually it is the person who asks you to consult the oracle. Occasionally, you will be asked to do a reading for someone who is not present, someone you have never met—in this case, find out as much as you can about the absent subject of the inquiry from those who are present. Even when you do a reading to inquire into the suitability or nature of a geographical place, or the meaning of a certain social or political situation, you are still doing the reading for someone, and that person cannot be discounted. They are an integral factor in the interpretation of the chart, because it is through the energy of their interest and desire that it is erected.

It might be thought at first consideration that runic astrology cannot be consulted at a distance through the mails or over the telephone due to the physical involvement of the querent in cutting the cards and blowing on the rune dice. Certainly it is best if the querent is present during the erection of the chart, but it is not essential. When consulting the oracle for someone at a distance, the diviner becomes the querent during the process of selecting the runes and placing the planets. This is done by learning as much as possible about the querent through a letter or phone conversation, then concentrating on both the querent and the question while shuffling the rune cards and casting the rune dice.

Once the chart is set up, it is read just as it would be if the querent had been present during its formation. A written report may then be sent by mail to the querent if the communication is through the post; if the link is by phone the diviner can interpret the large chart directly to the querent even as it is being erected, which allows the querent to ask any questions that may come to mind.

If you decide to read the oracle on a professional basis, the question of what to charge for a reading will arise. At one time it was asserted that true prophets never charged for their services, and those who did charge were necessarily inferior because the money they received tainted the purity of their vision. This opinion has some merit. Anyone who gives of their time and effort to another without charging for it is demonstrating a degree of altruism which in this modern material world might well qualify them for sainthood. However, most diviners who read for strangers do demand some compensation for their services.

The amount you may expect to receive is determined by market forces. The more in demand your services become, the more you will be paid. A good rule of thumb in the beginning is to ask for a sum in proportion to the labor you have put into the reading. A quick verbal reading from the large chart takes little time; a detailed, typed report accompanied by the small chart, in addition to the reading of the large chart, may require as much as several days to perform, and should command a proportionately higher sum. Inevitably, supply and demand will set the price.

Try to be optimistic when you interpret the oracle so that the querent will be able to use the information in your analysis in a positive way. If the reading is all negative, the querent will immediately become depressed and reject it without even trying to relate it to life circumstances. This does not mean you should misinterpret the chart—only that you should stress the useful and downplay the harmful. If the chart reveals a dangerous or destructive situation in the life of the querent, it is your obligation to reveal it in an accurate and complete manner, because this will be of service to the querent.

The sample life reading in chapter fifteen was chosen precisely because it is almost completely unfavorable. It shows how to say something constructive about a negative situation. It is your function as diviner to help the querent—that is why your services are sought, not to confuse with vague generalizations, or depress with evil tidings. Always bear this in mind when doing a reading for anyone, including yourself.

Your clients may ask you to perform a second divination on the same question immediately after the first in the hope of changing their fortune by changing the response of the oracle. Do not allow them to persuade you to repeat the reading. Second guessing the oracle yields nothing that is of value, and may actually result in great harm.

Any system of divination that depends on a randomizing factor, such as the I Ching, geomancy, the Tarot, and the runes, will give different results each time the divination is done. Astrologers regard this as proof that astrology is superior to these systems, because the positions of the planets and stars are always the same for a particular time and place, no matter how often that chart is cast or who casts it. They are less willing to acknowledge that the interpretation of this invariable pattern of the heavens will differ completely from astrologer to astrologer, depending on the background knowledge the astrologer possesses about the querent and the mental and emotional baggage the astrologer brings to the reading. Astrology has its own hidden randomizing factor—the wisdom, knowledge, understanding, attitude, and insight of the astrologer.

The variability that results from the shuffling of cards and the casting of dice can be looked upon as a strength rather than a weakness. It is the open window through which the hand of fate can reach and arrange the pattern of the oracle to represent the future with specific reference to a particular need and circumstance. Just as divine providence sets the stars in the heavens for any given instant, so does it control the sequence of the cards and the fall of the dice in runic astrology.

The purity and strength of the oracle stems from the unique point in space and the moment in time at which it occurs. An immediate subsequent reading is not a new and separate divination in its own right, but an attempt to verify, or amplify, or negate the original true divination. It may reveal interesting information concerning the expectations of the querent and the diviner, but will not be directly applicable to the question, as was the first working of the oracle.

Before conducting a second life reading for an individual, I would advise that you let at least a full year elapse. The passage of time changes the inner nature of a person and the outer life circumstances. Possibilities that existed at the time of the first reading will have either been fulfilled or lost, and a new array of possibilities will have arisen. To a large extent the second reading, done after a considerable lapse of time, will concern a different life.

You may work the oracle as many times as you wish for the same person, provided each working concerns a different question, but do not perform two readings close together in time for the same question. It is an insult to the oracle and an abuse of its power. The results of the second reading will be disappointing and misleading. If you persist in reading your own or someone else's life over and over, the response of the oracle will quickly become chaotic and even malicious. It is almost as though this trivial approach to the oracle angers the spiritual forces that direct it, and these spirits return contempt for contempt received.

Endnotes

Chapter One

1. Jung, 138.
2. Turner, 155.

Chapter Two

1. Tyson, *Rune Magic*, 17–27.
2. Ibid., 42; 69–73.
3. Barley, 49.
4. Regardie, *Golden Dawn*, 313.
5. Regardie, *Talismans*, 19.
6. Tyson, *New Millennium Magic*, 249–56.
7. Tyson, *Rune Magic*, 121–32.
8. Tyson, *Familiar Spirits*, 115–33.

Chapter Four

1. On the astrological significance of the order of the planets, see Ptolemy, 35–9.

Chapter Seven

1. George, 32.
2. Mayo, 97. On the various house systems of astrology, see Hone, 124–42.

Chapter Eight

1. Mann, 82.

Chapter Ten

1. Hone, 183.

Chapter Fourteen

1. Hone, 178–9. See also Mann, 192–5.
2. Mayo, 156.

Glossary

Aspect: An angle of separation between two astrological objects on the band of the zodiac, such as two planets, measured from the center of the horoscope. Only certain special regular angles are considered to form aspects, such as that of opposition (180 degrees), square (90 degrees), trine (60 degrees), semisquare (45 degrees), and so on.

Chart: A representation of the heavens used by astrologers to record the positions and aspects of the planets and other significant celestial objects, for the purposes of interpretation. It is sometimes called the horoscope. Rune astrology makes use of a large colored chart for display purposes, and small blank charts for recording the results of individual divinations.

Conjunction: Astrological aspect that exists when two planets or other significant objects in the chart are touching or very close together. In conventional astrology, objects are said to be in conjunction when they are separated by an angular distance of no more than 10 degrees, if either the Sun or Moon is involved—but the orb of separation is held to be 8 degrees if only the lesser lights are involved. For example, the Sun and Mars would be said to be in conjunction if they are separated by 9 degrees of arc on the zodiac, but Mars and Jupiter separated by the same 9 degrees would not be said to be in conjunction. In runic astrology, objects are said to be in conjunction when they lie on the same quine, or adjacent quines. This limits their separation to less than 10 degrees of arc.

Detriment: When a planet occupies a sign that is opposite the sign it naturally rules on the circle of the zodiac, it is said to be in detriment. For example, Mars is in detriment in

Libra, because Libra is opposite Aries on the zodiac, and Mars rules in Aries. A planet in detriment is weakened or hindered in its action.

Dignities: Positions occupied by planets in the zodiac that make their action more potent. There are five essential dignities, in decreasing order of importance: ruling sign, exaltation, triplicity, term, and face. Only the first two are of significance in runic astrology. There are two types of dignity—essential and accidental. An essential dignity is strength acquired by virtue of the location of the planet in the zodiac—certain zodiac positions are known as the essential dignities—whereas an accidental dignity is a position of increased strength that the planet occupies by accident of its position in the heavens at a given time and in relation to other factors in the chart.

Dragon's Head: The place where the ascending arc of the Moon's apparent path through the sky crosses the apparent path of the Sun, as observed from the surface of Earth. It is the point where the Moon passes from below the ecliptic to above the ecliptic. The Moon makes this crossing only once in its monthly cycle, but the node is considered to exist even when the Moon does not occupy it. It is called the Dragon's Head because the path traced through the heavens by the node appears to wind like the sinuous body of a dragon. It is known in Latin as *caput draconis*, and is also called the ascending node and the North Node.

Dragon's Tail: The place where the descending arc of the Moon's apparent path through the sky crosses the apparent path of the Sun, as observed from the surface of Earth. It is where the Moon passes downward through the ecliptic once in its monthly cycle, but this lunar node is considered to exist even when the Moon does not occupy it. *Cauda draconis* is its Latin name, and it is also called the South Node and the descending node of the Moon.

Ecliptic: In astrology, the circle that the Sun appears to trace through the heavens in the period of a year, as observed from Earth, and the plane in space defined by that circle, are known as the ecliptic. Where the Moon passes through the ecliptic in its monthly cycle, the ascending and descending lunar nodes are defined. The planets also have their nodes, but these are considered much less significant than the lunar nodes.

Elements: The philosophical or esoteric elements are usually considered to be four in number, and are called fire, water, air, and earth. There is a fifth element, called the quintessence, that underlies and vitalizes these more manifest four lower qualities of matter, but it is different in its nature and is often not referred to when the elements are named. In modern Western magic, the fifth element is known as spirit. The four lower, or earthly, elements are not tangible, but their natures are expressed by the tangible substances that bear their names. For example, the element water is not physical water, but physical water reveals the nature of the element water by its qualities and its behavior. In astrology, each zodiac sign is related to one of the four lower elements.

Exaltation: A planet in its sign of exaltation is strengthened in its working. The only stronger position for the planet is the sign it rules. Each planet has one sign of exaltation: Sun (Aries), Moon (Taurus), Mercury (Virgo), Venus (Pisces), Mars (Capricorn), Jupiter (Cancer), Saturn (Libra).

Fall: A planet is in fall when it occupies a sign of the zodiac that is opposite its sign of exaltation. For example, Mars is in fall in Cancer, because it is exalted in Capricorn, and Cancer is opposite Capricorn on the circle of the zodiac. Planets in fall are weak and somewhat frustrated in their actions. Since there is only one sign of exaltation for each planet, there is only one sign of fall for each planet.

Family: The twenty-four runes of the Old German *futhark* are divided into three groups of eight runes each, known as families. This division is ancient, and must have been considered quite important, since the three-fold structure was preserved even when the runes were reduced in number to sixteen in Scandinavia, and increased to thirty-three in England.

Futhark: The name of the Old German rune alphabet of twenty-four runes, derived from the sounds of the first six runes in the alphabet: F-U-Th-A-R-K. It is the most ancient of the rune alphabets, and the purest in an occult sense. It was being used for divination and purposes of practical magic in the time of Julius Caesar, and was already mature and fully formed at that time.

Grand Cross: A compound aspect formed when four or more planets or other significant astrological objects are arranged in square aspects, so that they define a great square, or cross, through the center of the chart. The square aspects enhance each other, creating a condition of conflict and general unease. A grand cross through cardinal signs indicates frustrations in bringing purposes to their fulfillment; through mutable signs, a lack of focus and vagueness in communications; through fixed signs, inertia and delay.

Grand Trine: A compound aspect formed when three or more planets or other significant astrological objects are arranged in trine aspects, so that they define the points of an equilateral triangle within the center of the chart. Each trine aspect intensifies the harmony of the others, creating a general climate of ease and freedom from strife.

Horary Astrology: A type of astrology in which a horoscope is cast at the time a question is asked, for the purpose of resolving that question. Rune astrology is not horary astrology, since it takes no account of the actual positions of the Ascendant, or the planets in the heavens, but it is similar in some aspects to horary astrology—for example, in its emphasis on the lunar nodes.

Horoscope: See Chart

Houses: A division of the zodiac into twelve parts that is based on time. Every day the earth makes one complete rotation on its axis. This moves the eastern horizon, known as the Ascendant degree, through the entire ring of the zodiac signs. Much of the meaning of astrology derives from where the Ascendant is at the moment for which a horoscope is cast, because it determines the relationship between the ring of the houses and the ring of the signs.

North Node: See Dragon's Head

Opposition: Major astrological aspect consisting of 180 degrees of arc. Planets or other significant objects are said to be in opposition when they are directly opposite each other on the horoscope.

Orb: An arc of angular distance that is used to determine whether two or more objects are in aspect. It is the deviation allowed by astrologers from a perfect aspect angle. For example, in conventional astrology two objects at 60 degrees to each other are in trine aspect, but if they are actually separated by an angle of 63 degrees they are still considered to be in trine aspect, because the orb of the trine aspect is (usually) held to be 4 degrees of arc. Different astrologers use various sizes for orbs, so it is difficult to be dogmatic in stating the size of orbs. Major aspects have larger orbs than minor aspects. In runic astrology, planets or other objects can only be placed with an accuracy of 5 degrees, so effectively all orbs, apart from that of the aspect of conjunction, are limited to the quines occupied by the objects. Conjunction is the exception—objects are in conjunction in runic astrology when on the same quine, or adjacent quines.

Querent: In astrology and in other forms of divination, the querent is the person asking the question the reading is about, or the one who seeks a life reading. The rune astrologer reads the chart for the querent.

Quincunx: A minor aspect of 150 degrees of arc. It is made up of the angular measure of five semisextile aspects, hence its name. It is sometimes known as the inconjunct aspect because any two signs in quincunx do not share the same polarity, quality, or elemental associations.

Quindecan: A division of 15 degrees of arc on the circle of the zodiac. There are twenty-four quindecans in all. Each sign has two quindecans.

Quine: A division of 5 degrees of arc on the circle of the zodiac. There are seventy-two quines in all. Each sign has six quines.

Rule: A planet is said to rule the sign in which that planet is most at home. All the planets rule two signs, except the Sun, which rules only Leo, and the Moon, which rules only Cancer. The action of a planet is strongest in its own sign. Planetary rule is the greatest of the five essential dignities.

Runes: A set of simple symbols that evolved among the Teutonic tribes of northern Europe centuries before the time of Christ, which was used both for written communication and for works of divination and magic. No one is certain how or when the runes were created, but it is conjectured that they were inspired by the Etruscan alphabet, when Teutonic barbarians crossed the Alps to fight in what is now northern Italy. A fusion occurred between the Etruscan letters and the occult symbols being employed by northern shamans that resulted in the runes. The Greek and Latin alphabets may also have had some influence on the shape of some of the runes. In the mythology of the ancient Germans, it was the god Wotan who snatched up the runes from the roots of the world ash tree, Yggdrasill, and gave them to his followers.

Semisextile: Minor astrological aspect of 30 degrees, one-half of the sextile aspect.

Semisquare: As the name suggests, this minor astrological aspect is one-half that of the square, or 45 degrees.

Sesquiquadrate: Minor aspect of 135 degrees that signifies a minor degree of stress. It is formed by the combination of the angular measures of the square aspect and semisquare aspect.

Sextile: Major astrological aspect of 60 degrees that is considered to be harmonious and beneficent.

Signs: The zodiac is divided into twelve equal parts, called signs, each of which has its own related archetypal figure and area of influence. The signs are Aries, Taurus, Gemini, Cancer,

Leo, Virgo, Libra, Scorpio, Sagittarius, Capricorn, Aquarius, and Pisces. Closely related to the signs are the houses, a similar division of the zodiac into twelve parts based on the duration of Earth's rotation.

South Node: See Dragon's Tail.

Square: Major astrological aspect of 90 degrees, in which objects are placed at right angles to each other on the chart, as measured from its center. A square aspect indicates difficulties.

T-Square: A compound aspect that is formed when two planets or other objects in opposition are in square aspect with a third object. The general tension created by opposition is aggravated by the influence of the square.

Trine: Major astrological aspect of 120 degrees, the most harmonious of all aspects.

Zodiac: An imaginary band of the heavens that extends 8 degrees above and 8 degrees below the plane of the ecliptic. It may be conceived as a great invisible ribbon in space that wraps completely around the earth. The path of the Sun across the sky traces the centerline of this circle of ribbon, which is divided into twelve equal parts, each with its own mythological associations.

Bibliography

Agrippa, Henry C. *Henry Cornelius Agrippa, His Fourth Book of Occult Philosophy* [1655]. Edited and translated by Robert Turner. London: Askin Publishers, 1978.

Barley, Alfred H. *The Rationale of Astrology.* London: Lyncroft Gardens, 1905.

George, Llewellyn. *A To Z Horoscope Maker and Delineator.* St. Paul, MN: Llewellyn Publications, 1968.

Hone, Margaret E. *The Modern Text Book of Astrology.* London: L. N. Fowler & Co. Ltd, 1951.

Jones, Marc Edmund. *The Guide To Horoscope Interpretation*, Philadelphia, PA: David McKay, 1941.

Jung, Carl. *C. G. Jung Letters, Volume One 1906–1950.* Translated by R. F. C. Hull. London: Routledge and Kegan Paul, 1973.

Mann, A. T. *The Round Art: The Astrology of Time and Space.* New York: Mayflower Books, 1979.

Mayo, Jeff. *Astrology* [1964]. London: The English Universities Press Ltd., 1970.

Ptolemy. *Tetrabiblos.* Edited and translated by F. E. Robbins. Cambridge, MA: Harvard University Press; London: William Heinmann Ltd., 1980.

Regardie, Israel. *How To Make and Use Talismans* [1971]. Revised ed. Wellingborough, Northamptonshire: Aquarian Press, 1981.

Regardie, Israel. *The Golden Dawn*, 6th ed. St. Paul, MN: Llewellyn Publications, 1989.

Tyson, Donald. *Familiar Spirits: A Practical Guide for Witches and Magicians.* St. Paul, MN: Llewellyn Publications, 2004.

Tyson, Donald. *New Millennium Magic: A Complete System of Self-Realization.* St. Paul, MN: Llewellyn Publications, 1996.

————. *Rune Dice.* Kit containing a set of four rune dice, plus the book *Rune Dice Divination.* St. Paul, MN: Llewellyn Publications, 1997.

————. *Rune Magic.* St. Paul, MN: Llewellyn Publications, 1988.

————. *Three Books of Occult Philosophy by Henry Cornelius Agrippa of Nettesheim.* Donald Tyson, editor. St. Paul, MN: Llewellyn Publications, 1993.

Index

To Write to the Author

If you wish to contact the author or would like more information about this book, please write to the author in care of Llewellyn Worldwide and we will forward your request. Both the author and publisher appreciate hearing from you and learning of your enjoyment of this book and how it has helped you. Llewellyn Worldwide cannot guarantee that every letter written to the author can be answered, but all will be forwarded. Please write to:

Donald Tyson
⅍ Llewellyn Worldwide
2143 Wooddale Drive, Dept. 978-0-7387-1506-3
Woodbury, Minnesota 55125-2989, U.S.A.
Please enclose a self-addressed stamped envelope for reply,
or $1.00 to cover costs. If outside U.S.A., enclose
international postal reply coupon.

Many of Llewellyn's authors have Web sites with additional information and resources. For more information, please visit our Web site at http://www.llewellyn.com

1-2-3 Tarot

Answers in an Instant

DONALD TYSON

Reading Tarot has never been easier! Most Tarot instruction books require readers to memorize the keywords of each card—quite a challenge for those who've never held a Tarot deck before. Donald Tyson takes the burden off beginners by providing a whole new approach to Tarot that's easy and effective.

A card's complex significance is boiled down to three elements: identity, action, and result/quality. When these elements are matched respectively with a subject, verb, and object, they form a simple sentence and give succinct meaning to the card. Donald Tyson teaches how to interpret the collective meaning of three-card sets within a variety of spreads. Flexible, fast, and fun, this foolproof system can be applied to all decks.

978-0-7387-0527-9, 264 pp., 6 x 9   **$12.95**

Runic Palmistry

A Norse Method of Divination

JON SAINT-GERMAIN

This unique book combines standard palmistry, Norse mythology, and the runes, using all three to understand a person and his or her path, personality, needs and special gifts.

It is a system handed down orally through four generations of Jon Saint-Germain's family, originally learned from a mysterious Scandinavian who entered the family circle two hundred years ago. In this system, lines of the palm are called "branches," and mounts of the palm are named after Norse deities. You will learn the meanings of the fingers in the light of exciting Norse mythology. This is the only book on the subject available.

978-1-56718-577-5, 240 pp., 7½ x 9⅛   **$14.95**

A Practical Guide to the Runes
Their Uses in Divination and Magick

LISA PESCHEL

At last the world has a beginner's book on the Nordic runes that is written in straightforward and clear language. Each of the twenty-five runes is elucidated through no-nonsense descriptions and clean graphics. A rune's altered meaning in relation to other runes and its reversed position is also included. The construction of runes and accessories covers such factors as the type of wood to be used, the size of the runes, and the coloration, carving, and charging of the runes.

With this book the runes can be used in magick to effect desired results. Talismans carved with runescripts or bindrunes allow you to carry your magick in a tangible form, providing foci for your will. Four rune layouts complete with diagrams are presented with examples of specific questions to ask when consulting the runes. Rather than simple fortunetelling devices, the runes are oracular, empowered with the forces of Nature. They present information for you to make choices in your life.

978-0-87542-593-1, 192 pp., 4¾₆ x 6⅞   **$6.99**

Divination for Beginners

Reading the Past, Present & Future

SCOTT CUNNINGHAM

There's no need to visit a soothsayer or call a psychic hotline to glimpse into your future or to uncover your past. You can become your own diviner of things unseen with the many methods outlined in this book, written by popular author Scott Cunningham.

Here you will find detailed descriptions of both common and unusual divinatory techniques, each grouped by the tools or techniques used to perform them. Many utilize natural forces such as water, clouds, smoke, and the movement of birds. Also discussed are the more advanced techniques of Tarot, Palmistry, and the I Ching.

978-0-7387-0384-2, 264 pp., 5³⁄₁₆ x 8   **$11.95**

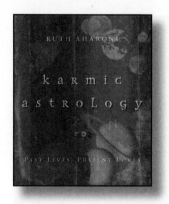

Karmic Astrology

Past Lives, Present Loves

RUTH AHARONI

Is there a karmic connection that binds us to the closest people in our lives? If so, how can we gain insight from past incarnations? Perhaps the answers to these mind-boggling riddles lie in the stars.

In *Karmic Astrology*, Ruth Aharoni demonstrates how to learn from the karmic "footprints" visible in an astrological birth chart. She identifies the distinctive karmic characteristics found in the astrological signs, planets, aspects, houses, nodes, and elements. This groundbreaking book can help readers identify karmic partners, understand why a particular mate was chosen, and improve current relations with friends, family members, and spouses. In addition to valuable relationship insight, this book also provides advice and meditations for attracting a soul mate.

978-0-7387-0967-3, 192 pp., 7½ x 9⅛   **$14.95**